Rock Doctrine

Rock Doctrine

A Biblical Theology of God's Presence
through Stone Imagery

Greg Anthony Crawford
Foreword by Jason Alligood

WIPF & STOCK · Eugene, Oregon

ROCK DOCTRINE
A Biblical Theology of God's Presence through Stone Imagery

Copyright © 2024 Greg Anthony Crawford. All rights reserved. Except for brief quotations in critical publications or reviews, no part of this book may be reproduced in any manner without prior written permission from the publisher. Write: Permissions, Wipf and Stock Publishers, 199 W. 8th Ave., Suite 3, Eugene, OR 97401.

Wipf & Stock
An Imprint of Wipf and Stock Publishers
199 W. 8th Ave., Suite 3
Eugene, OR 97401

www.wipfandstock.com

PAPERBACK ISBN: 979-8-3852-0434-2
HARDCOVER ISBN: 979-8-3852-0435-9
EBOOK ISBN: 979-8-3852-0436-6

VERSION NUMBER 06/27/24

Unless otherwise indicated, all Scripture quotations are from the ESV® Bible (The Holy Bible, English Standard Version®), © 2001 by Crossway, a publishing ministry of Good News Publishers. Used by permission. All rights reserved. The ESV text may not be quoted in any publication made available to the public by a Creative Commons license. The ESV may not be translated in whole or in part into any other language.

Scripture quotations taken from the (NASB®) New American Standard Bible®, Copyright © 1960, 1971, 1977, 1995 by the Lockman Foundation. Used by permission. All rights reserved. lockman.org.

Some content taken from *The Babylonian Talmud* by Jacob Neusner. Copyright © 2011. Used by permission of Hendrickson Rose Publishing Group, represented by Tyndale House Publishers. All rights reserved.

To Katie, Macey, Isaac, and Jackson, with love.

Contents

Foreword by Jason Alligood | ix
Acknowledgments | xi
Abbreviations | xv

Introduction | 1
1 The Rock: Jesus Christ | 8
2 The Rock: The Temple | 17
3 The Rock: The Mountain of God | 27
4 The Rock: God | 41
5 The Rock: The King | 52
6 The Rock: The Kingdom | 64
7 The Rock: Foundation of New Testament Christology | 78
8 The Rock: Foundation of New Testament Ecclesiology | 96
9 Pastoral Insights | 114

Bibliography | 121
Ancient Document Index | 129

Foreword

THE BIBLE IS UNLIKE any other book ever written. It is the only book written by forty plus authors over thousands of years and yet can carry the claim that it is also written by a Triune God who superintended its human authors. It is not only full of historical data like the events of the Israelite people and most importantly pointing us to Jesus and how we may be reconciled to God, through his perfect life, death, and resurrection, but also full of metaphorical language that points to the very same thing. The last few decades scholars have produced myriads of material tracing these biblical–theological themes throughout the Scriptures. Books abound concerning the metaphorical and analogical language of serpents, temple, water, trees, and generally the big picture of creation, fall, redemption, and consummation. There is a world's library worth of reading in the genre. And yet, one emblem that needs more stones overturned is found in the project you are currently holding (pun fully intended!). Yet, you may still wonder: what hath geology to do with Jesus?

Perhaps you're picking up this book with a tinge of curiosity because of the title. Or perhaps *Rock Doctrine* got you excited because you imagined this work was a crossover between theology and the various iterations of the monumental Christian rock band Petra (God did give rock 'n' roll to you, after all). Well, let me assure you, though that would be an incredible book, what you hold in your hands is more epic and more important!

If you are familiar with the Bible, you no doubt know that stones appear throughout its pages. Just a quick jaunt through your Bible knowledge will bring back memories of "stones of remembrance" and the rock of the wilderness which Moses eventually disobeyed and struck instead of following God's instruction, the same rock to which Paul points and says is Jesus, or how Jesus himself rolls away the stone which covers his own grave. And

Foreword

you would be right in your short reassessment and in the final couple of examples you may begin to see that at which this book aims. However, in this volume, Greg Crawford takes us beyond our mere Sunday school or yearly Bible-reading memories and deftly traces the biblical-theological metaphor of rock and stone imagery throughout the Scriptures to give us an accounting of why this motif is so important to our understanding of who our Triune God is and how we ought to grow deeper in our understanding of him and as a result worship him more.

Nothing could be more important for those of us who are in Christ than to plumb the depths of the Bible and squeeze every last drop of meaning from its pages, and Greg Crawford helps us in bringing to light another aspect of its truth by which we do not merely gain more knowledge of our Lord Jesus Christ, but are enriched in our desire to know him and his truth even more as we await his return.

    Jason Alligood
    Assistant Professor of Theology
    Cedarville University

Acknowledgments

A PHILOSOPHICAL ARGUMENT COULD be made that just about everyone who has ever lived has a right to the list of influencers upon this work. Friends, family, neighbors I've never met, and people on the other side of the ocean, are all part of a global network that ebbs and flows in the wake of everyday words, behaviors, and interactions. This means the dollars I spend, the technology I use, and the coffee I drink—all very essential components for completing this project—are indebted to everyone everywhere to some degree. Working backward in history, this fact is no different. Remove one person in history-past from the chain of cause and effect, and the circumstances which led me to this very point may have never materialized. But while these indirect influences—and unknown direct influences—are certainly responsible for the shape of the content of this work, it is the known direct influences who I desire to honor in this section.

To begin, I would like to thank Wipf and Stock publishers for recognizing the merit of the concept for which I write. I'm also thankful that they were willing to take a chance on a "first-timer," as this is my first published book. A special thanks goes out to Matthew Wimer for guiding me through the publishing process and using his valuable time to answer the assortment of questions that I had as I charted this new terrain.

I am a firm believer that theology never happens in a vacuum. Therefore, I would like to acknowledge several people that have regularly helped me shape my ideas and the overall hermeneutic I've developed for seeing biblical themes unfold. At the most personal level, I'd like to thank my friends, Chris Cooper and Brad Harris, for always being available to field questions, give feedback, and challenge assumptions. These pastor-theologians have helped shape me for the last two decades and their influence on my theology, and life generally speaking, cannot be overstated.

Acknowledgments

Next I would like to thank Dr. Brian Koning for being readily available to help me navigate some of the minutiae within Hebrew scholarship. There were several times throughout the writing of this work that a late-night obstacle threatened to bring the writing process to a halt. Brian's knowledge and insight into the world of Old Testament studies rescued me from hours of personal investigation that was otherwise outside the scope of my arguments. For that I am truly thankful.

I would also like to thank my two encouragers, Jason Sisemore and Dr. Jason Alligood, for investing in this process. Both of these men took time to read and respond to portions of this book as it was being pieced together. There were times in the writing process where I got so overly familiar with the work that I lost the ability to evaluate it objectively. These men were a fresh set of eyes ensuring that the flow of thought was coherent and profitable for the reader. Furthermore, these men have been a general encouragement to me as long as I've known them. I cannot overstate how their kind words and actions have led me to the confidence necessary to move forward in this literary endeavor.

One of the primary reasons this book came to fruition was because of the encouraging feedback I received after preaching over the *rock* in Matthew. The people of Living Water Church were thirsty to drink from this theological fountain, which inspired me to go even further into the study than a Sunday morning sermon series would permit. The countless people who have prayed for me, encouraged me, challenged me, and walked with me during the process, have truly effected the trajectory of these ideas, and for that I'm truly thankful.

Being that the cornerstone stands as a central focus of this book, I cannot forget the foundations upon which I stand. Therefore, I would like to thank my parents, Dale and Joyce Crawford, for being an early foundational stone of my theological scholarship. Their love for Jesus and his word was instilled in me as a youth and is now a motivating force behind all that I preach, teach, and write.

And finally, I must acknowledge my wonderful family for the sacrifices they make to bring my efforts to completion. To my wife, Katie, I thank you for holding down the fort every time I needed to slip away to conduct research, think, write, or collaborate with others on the project. Hundreds of hours were poured into this book, which means you spent hundreds of hours wrestling three kids, homeschooling, running a business, and maintaining order in the home, with no help from me. You are

Acknowledgments

the *capable woman* of Prov 31, and I appreciate your commitment and contribution toward this book. To my children, Macey, Isaac, and Jackson, I am thankful for your sacrifice as well. You have endured periods of time where I have been physically absent, but have, more importantly, put up with my mental absence. God only knows how many times you attempted to interact with me but were unsuccessful because I was deep in thought regarding the "next chapter," a "better ending," or some other aspect of this project. My prayer is that you and others will be blessed by the contents of this book and that you can recognize the valuable part you played in bringing it to completion.

Abbreviations

ANE	Ancient Near East
b.	Babylonian Talmud
BDAG	W. Bauer, W. F. Arndt, F. W. Gingrich, and F. W. Danker. *A Greek-English Lexicon of the New Testament and Other Early Christian Literature.* 3rd ed.
DSS	Dead Sea Scrolls
ESV	English Standard Version
LXX	Septuagint
NASB	New American Standard Bible
NT	New Testament
OT	Old Testament
YHWH	Yahweh

Introduction

THE BIBLE IS A book about rocks. There are, of course, other motifs that are traceable through Scripture but none are insulated from "rock theology." As one canvases the high points of the biblical storyline, it is impossible to ignore the presence of rocks within its plot, setting, and overarching theology. This observation can be seen through the way authors frequently utilize figurative language wherein stone metaphors serve the purpose of communicating certain attributes of God to his people. Additionally, rocks serve as bookends to the broader narrative of Scripture, with the opening chapters of Genesis and the closing chapters of Revelation containing references to theological stones. Within these parenthetical bookends are descriptions of rocks as physical centerpieces to the sacred spaces of divine communication between God and humanity (Gen 28:18; Exod 31:18; 33:22; Deut 10:2–5; 1 Kgs 8:9; 1 Chr 22:2). Furthermore, rocks and stones show up in the biblical record as instruments of deliverance for the Israelites in battle (Exod 17:12; 1 Sam 17:50), and they often depict God's victorious reign over the various powers of the world (2 Sam 22:3; Dan 2:31–45).

Even more important than their abundant presence in the biblical storyline, rocks carry theological significance as they appear in Scripture. When Jesus speaks of building one's house upon the rock, predicts that he will build his church upon the rock, and references himself as the cornerstone, he is revealing more than the observable attributes of rocks can tell. Jesus uses such language because his immediate audience recognizes the theological ties embedded within this imagery. By using the word "rock," Jesus reveals more about his kingdom and his own identity than a thousand words could convey.

Unfortunately for the modern reader, these seemingly obvious correlations and allusions are sometimes missed. Our distinct culture removes us from the intuitive ability to connect lines of thought and develop word associations that were second nature to a first-century Israelite. Their exposure to rabbinical teaching in the synagogue, the agricultural environment within which they worked and lived, and the state of development and infrastructure within Palestine, each served to reinforce the significance of rocks and stone within the ancient Jewish worldview. Two thousand years later, many students of the Bible have little exposure to rabbinical teaching and live urban lifestyles within which rock and stone are aesthetically blended into, and hidden within, the synthetic tapestry of modern development. Consequently, today's reader stands little chance of gleaning from these rock metaphors without exploring the biblical and cultural backgrounds surrounding the terminology.

PURPOSE

The aim of this book is to show the reader that the rock metaphor is loaded with theological implications that are utilized in the NT's development of Christology and ecclesiology. By tapping the OT's engagement with the symbol, the ideas of temple, priesthood, divinity, kingship, kingdom, and numerous other features can be detected in the portrait of Christ and his church. However, these features do not appear in Scripture abruptly or simultaneously but are subtly developed over time. The way in which these features emerge is another prominent focus of this book, as it is delightful to not only watch *what* God does, but to see *how* he does it.

METHODOLOGY

To explore this motif, a pathway must be established to avoid the insurmountable number of theological obstacles that could distract from the primary purpose. The intention of the book is to draw connections within God's word to formulate a clear and concise biblical theology of the rock motif which means any debates surrounding authorship or textual criticism lie outside the scope of this work. The Bible will be treated as a work of inspiration, where both human and divine authorship is assumed, and will be regularly quoted and alluded to as it appears in its final form within the Protestant tradition.

This book will introduce the reader to the progression of the rock theme and connect significant points of interest throughout the biblical narrative. These points of connection will demonstrate how each biblical author built upon theological statements and ideas from past revelation and will provide an overview of the trajectory rock theology took as it spanned the various eras of biblical writing. The *borrowing* and *building* hermeneutic of the OT epitomizes how the NT writers arrive at their conclusions. By the time they write, an entire system of scaffolding has been erected upon which their Christology and ecclesiology can be established.

The Metaphor

Metaphors are a premier feature of biblical literature and deserve a brief introduction before delving into the specific passages within which they arise in this study. When the Bible suggests that someone, or something, is a rock, it is rarely the case that they are being described as a *solid mass of aggregated minerals*. The statement, more often than not, is a comparison of two things from which an evaluation is derived for a meaningful proposition. For example, when God is described as a rock, the reader is asked to access the database of what they know about God and rocks respectively. A comparison is then made to deduce which of the matching attributes is being highlighted by the metaphor to describe God.

Though the mechanics of the metaphor appear quite simple, a couple of complexities arise in the process. First, the proper interpretation of the metaphor assumes a degree of understanding on the part of the reader regarding the two subjects being compared, yet each reader will likely arrive at the literature with a different set of presuppositions. If their experiences tell them that rocks are durable, useful for building, dangerous in certain situations, and nonliving, then their presuppositions about God will dictate which qualities are intended by the metaphor, and which are not. However, not everyone comes to the biblical record with the same presuppositions regarding God, nor do they each have the same experiences with rocks. The combination of outcomes for interpreting the metaphor, then, are numerous. While one might interpret the metaphor as describing God's *strength*, another might view the comparison as a way of describing God's *inactivity* in the world. Yet, the Bible has not extended a license for multiple interpretations based on the diversity of its readership but, rather, requires that the reader acknowledge the intentions of the author who made the comparison. This demands that the reader share a common understanding with the author regarding both topics in the metaphorical comparison.

This brings us to the second complexity of interpreting metaphors; the necessity of thinking about each subject *like the author*. Since the author created the metaphor with certain qualities in mind, the reader's duty is to discover that which was intended. This does not, however, require that the reader know *everything* about God and rocks that the author knew. Rather, it requires that the reader discover the features of the metaphor that the author assumed would be easily recognized by the audience to which he wrote. This process goes well beyond recognizing the general concepts existent within the author's databank, since the writer rarely intends to compare *all* the features of rocks that he is aware of to *all* the known qualities of God. It is usually one specific attribute, or a web of interrelated qualities, that surface in the use of the metaphor. Through examining the grammatical content surrounding the metaphor, the history of the metaphor's usage, and the theological worldview of the writer and his audience, these specific intentions of the author can be derived with a high degree of certainty.

The metaphor, then, must be explored based on the mutual understanding of the writer and his audience. Any understanding of God, or the other subjects being compared to the rock through the use of the metaphor, that does not align with the theological contour of the biblical record will fail to properly grasp the intended meaning of the author. Furthermore, an incomplete understanding of the rock and the theological shape it takes in the Jewish mind also hinders the interpretive process. Like many words in our own culture, a certain degree of "baggage" may be attached to terms that would be otherwise absent in other historical contexts. Yet, a failure to acknowledge the meaning carried by these associations is a misstep in communication when these overtones were clearly intended by the person using the word. In the same way, if today's reader does not acknowledge the theological developments of the rock in Scripture, the use of the metaphor falls flat on modern ears.

OUTLINE

Chapter 1 will introduce the rock motif by examining the various places rocks and stones are used in relation to Jesus and his ministry. The numerous statements tying Christ to the rock reveal the importance of grasping its theological significance and are helpful in constructing the christological picture the biblical authors intended to portray. Looking at the assortment

Introduction

of texts invites the reader to examine the theological load embedded within the rock metaphor.

Chapter 2 will begin the process of assembling the material from which the NT naturally borrowed; a collection of ideas, metaphors, and allusions from the OT that have come to be known as the *rock* or *stone testimonia*.[1] The starting point for this process is exploring the connection between Christ and the temple. The theologically charged reference to the "cornerstone," a designation for Christ in the NT, was originally penned within descriptions of the temple sanctum and became a symbolic representation of the temple in later Judaism. These sections of Scripture alluding to the cornerstone of the temple are typically within the literary context of divine protection and judgement which parallel the way Christ is portrayed through the use of rock terminology. While the cornerstone functioned as a rock of security for the believer, it became a stone of stumbling for the wicked. In comparison, Christ's instruction revealed a similar fate for those opposing his message, while simultaneously offering a guarantee of enduring security for his church.

The next chapter will look backwards chronologically at the cornerstone motif and explore the mountain of God as another significant concept within the OT's stone testimonia. Three particular mountains will be evaluated as antecedents to the rock metaphor, the first being Zion. This mountain served as the geological foundation upholding Solomon's temple, and hence, receives a share in the identification of the "cornerstone." Yet, many of the theological ties to Zion were developed from earlier iterations of the *mountain of God*. Sinai and Eden are both referred to as a divine mountain and served as points of communication between heaven and earth. The temple's function is likely developed from these antecedent descriptions, making them a point of interest for understanding the progression of the stone testimonia.

Chapter 4 shifts from actual stone formations of the OT to the theological concept of God-as-rock. Numerous passages describe YHWH as the rock or as a rock structure (e.g., fortress). These designations provide insight into why the rock formations highlighted in the previous chapters became so important for the Jews. God's presence and communication at these stone-locations infused the actual material with meaning and significance. The rocks have no theological value in and of themselves, and many

---

1. See Snodgrass, "Christological Stone Testimonia"; and more recently, Freeman, "Church's One Foundation."

lose what value they once had as the storyline progresses, but those places esteemed as sacred are always made so by the presence of YHWH.

The fifth chapter will explore the king as a figure who receives the rock designation. As a representative of God's presence, the king was intended to reflect the rule of YHWH over Israel. In light of the many failures recorded in Israel's monarchy, the primary references to the royal rock are messianic. The prophets envisioned a day where a king would arise from the house of David and would restore the temple and the kingdom. The way the Psalms and the Prophets employed the rock testimonia became significant in the theological developments of the intertestamental period, as well as the NT era, as the kingdom and temple began to converge in the messianic portrait.

Chapter 6 moves from the description of the king to the metaphorical use of rock to describe the kingdom. Though a king was prophesied to come, the OT also described the *kingdom* of God in language that incorporated it into the rock testimonia. Daniel is a primary source for engaging this topic, since he depicts a rock that destroys the other kingdoms but then grows into a mountain that encompasses the entire world. Many of the NT uses of the rock metaphor rely on the theological assumptions present in these images for christological and ecclesiological development.

The seventh chapter will return to the NT to apply the discoveries of the previous chapters to Jesus' fulfillment of the rock motif and to draw a number of christological implications. By this point, the NT reader should recognize that the rock is a literary reference infused with deep theological meaning. The ways in which the NT writers engage with the rock testimonia draw from the preloaded image and apply varying aspects of theology to the Christ. Jesus's identity and purpose are developed by the NT writers' dependence on the OT and its theological commitments to the rock.

Chapter 8 will explore how the NT's Christology gives way to ecclesiology. The various truths that are deciphered through the NT's engagement with the rock testimonia are directly related to the depiction of the church. The ways in which Jesus fulfills the predictions of the rock are pivotal to the church's identity. The faith community is described as the temple of God and is compelled to operate as priests in the fallen world. Simultaneously, the rock imagery advances the narrative of dominion that was initially present in Eden. Through Christ, the church has regained its purpose to fulfill the priest-king mission of filling the world with divine image bearers who submit to the king.

Introduction

    The final chapter is a brief sketch of the primary implications of this research. After eight chapters of academic exploration of the rock metaphor, this chapter is written from a pastoral perspective to demonstrate the significance of these theological findings in the daily life of the Christian and the church respectively.

    The goal of this project is not only to draw attention to an undertreated motif of biblical theology, but to emphasize the church's unique place within the biblical storyline. The rock theme demonstrates, as clear as any analogy, the doctrine of *union with Christ* and gives the Christian believer confidence of their new identity. Additionally, this project, and others like it, demonstrates the continuity that exists between the OT and NT and between the individual writers within these respective canons. While many have undertaken projects to expose the distinctions between individual writers, and even between OT and NT theology, this book will help reinforce the idea of a common divine authorship that underlays the entire biblical narrative. Finally, I hope this literary contribution will fuel the fire beneath the student of Scripture to continue digging in the richness of God's word. There is much left to be discovered and taught. There are facets left to be polished and presented. There are blind spots needing to be revealed. May God use this work as motivation for all who delight in Scripture and seek to advance the truth hidden therein.

1

The Rock: Jesus Christ

IN THE INTRODUCTION, IT was said that the Bible is a book about rocks. But even the casual reader of Scripture would likely summarize the Bible as a book about God. Reconciling these two statements is hardly difficult when one surveys the variety of biblical texts linking God to rock and stone. The NT, however, suggests that the Bible is a book about Jesus and that all the OT points to him.[1] Furthermore, the various rock metaphors that were previously applied to God suddenly become a tool of the NT writer for describing the Messiah and his church. Between the opening chapter of Matthew and the concluding verse of Revelation, Jesus is referred to as the *cornerstone* no less than seven times.[2] Similarly, he is depicted as a rock of offense, a stone of stumbling, a foundation stone, a living stone, and the rock by which all Israel drank in the wilderness (Rom 9:33; 1 Cor 3:11; 10:4; 1 Pet 2:6–8). Revelation 2:17 reveals one of the many rewards for those who conquer through faith: "A white stone with a new name written on the stone." The record of Jesus' burial and resurrection sear images of stone into the minds of the reader through the vivid account of the stone tomb (Luke 23:53) and the stone that was rolled in place to seal the Messiah in death (Luke 24:2). The removal of the stone on resurrection Sunday has become

---

1. This was Jesus' interpretation in Luke 24:27; see Vanhoozer, *Drama of Doctrine*, 195.

2. Though there are two different Greek expressions being used, *kephalē gōnias* and *akrogōniaion*, the expressions are often used interchangeably and are indicative of the same truths. See "Stone, Cornerstone" in Martin and Davids, *Dictionary*, 1126–29.

The Rock: Jesus Christ

a central theme of celebration in numerous Christian hymns, dramatizations, and works of art.

Certainly, the authors of Scripture relied on rock imagery to describe Jesus and his ministry but it is worth noting that Jesus used rocks to describe himself and to illustrate the theological ideas he preached. His stories, parables, and object lessons relied heavily on earthen material. He taught in Matt 7 that a wise man builds his house upon the rock in juxtaposition to the fool who builds on the sand. He would go on to teach that his church would be built upon the rock and that the gates of hades would not defeat it. He condemned the fate of those who cause believers to stumble by saying it would be better for them if a millstone—a large circular rock used for grinding grain—were tied around their neck and they were drowned in the sea (Matt 18:6). The examples are plentiful but this sampling suffices to illustrate the abundant use of rock imagery in the teaching ministry of Jesus.

While the significance of rocks within the ministry of Christ is easily observable, it is not always understandable. In other words, we see the *quantity* of rock terminology, but often neglect the *quality* it brings to the theological narrative. The remaining sections of this chapter will flesh out some of these occurrences mentioned above and initiate a biblical-theological exploration of the rock motif in Scripture to highlight the qualitative texture these metaphors and allusions provide. This content will provide a starting point for moving chronologically backward through the Scripture to explore how rock imagery morphed and progressed in God's revelation and, thus, in the imaginary of those receiving these texts. In following this progression, it is my desire to highlight not only the meaning these correlations carry as they land in their NT context, but also the process that brings them to fruition. It is my conviction that process cannot, and should not, be disentangled from interpretation.

MATTHEW

The Gospel of Matthew serves as an ideal starting point. His writing is assumed by many scholars to be aimed at a Jewish audience and his interaction with OT texts and themes provide the exact literary environment desired for pursuing an investigation like the one being proposed.[3] Throughout Matthew, there are references and allusions to the rock motif of the OT that are contextualized to the person and ministry of Christ. Jesus' interaction

---

3. See Quarles, *Theology of Matthew*, 10–12.

with the rock thematically reveals much about his identity and provides the NT reader with a hermeneutical lens for establishing a rich Christology.

Towards the conclusion of the Sermon on the Mount in Matt 7:24–27, Jesus describes a scenario within which two outcomes are starkly contrasted. He states that there was a "wise man who built his house upon the rock" and a "foolish man who built his house upon the sand." In this story, the house upon the rock withstands the rain, wind, and floods brought about by the storm but the house built upon the sand falls and is utterly destroyed. This passage has frequently been used to illustrate the distinct eschatological outcomes between believers and unbelievers and to illustrate the indestructible nature of Christian faith.[4] These elements are certainly present in the context of Matt 7, however, little attention has been given to Matthew's greater awareness of rock theology and the OT passages that undergird these images.

While anyone familiar with homebuilding understands that a solid foundation is key to the longevity of a house, Jesus equates the security of the home with the hearing and doing of his words. It is likely that these instructions are derived from the Mosaic instruction in the Torah, specifically Deut 4, where *hearing* and *doing* establish the basis for covenantal faithfulness among the Israelites.[5] The Hebrew word for *hear* or *listen*, *Shema*, became a significant idea in Hebraic thought and implied the necessity of obedience or action to follow the hearing of God's commands. Numerous scholars have noted Matthew's portrait of Jesus as the new Moses in the Sermon on the Mount, therefore, it is not surprising that Jesus utilizes a Mosaic literary convention to instruct the new community of faith he is assembling.[6] While these connections are fascinating in and of themselves, what is of greatest importance is the correlations Moses' instructions have to being among the covenant community. Those who refuse to *listen* and *do* will perish and be driven from the promised land since they have broken covenant with God

---

4. Cf. Clifton, *Matthew and Mark*, 122–23; Henry and Scott, "Matt 7:21–29," in *Henry's Concise Commentary*.

5. See Floyd, "Concept of Discipleship in Deuteronomy," 37–71.

6. Jesus' ascent up "the mountain" and his sermon on the Beatitudes both reflect Moses' ascent up Sinai and the Decalogue that he received from God. Furthermore, the Decalogue came as stipulations that would bring about blessings for obedience or a curse for rebellion. The use of the phrase "blessed" in the beatitudes further connects Jesus to the Mosaic tradition. See France, *Gospel of Matthew*, 156–58, and Quarles, *Theology of Matthew*, 33–72.

(Deut 4:25–28).[7] Similarly, Jesus' audience will experience salvation or destruction depending on whether or not they *listen to* and *do* the words of Christ. In summary, listening and doing equate to being in covenant relationship with God which equate to being on the rock of salvation.

While these connections are somewhat subtle in Matt 7, they begin to expand and reveal Matthew's intentionality in employing rock theology in later chapters. Jesus' monumental statement in Matt 16:18 reads, "And I tell you, you are Peter, and on this rock I will build my church, and the gates of hell shall not prevail against it." Just like the earlier reference to the rock in Matt 7, Jesus once again employs building imagery where the rock serves as the foundation. While it has been hotly debated as to whether this rock is a reference to Peter, whose name literally means rock, or to Peter's confession, the word-picture used conveys another situation where protection from a hostile threat is needed and provided through the rock-based structure. While the threat in Matt 7 was described through the metaphor of *storm,* chapter 16 describes the threat as the *gates of hades*. The structure withstanding this threat is Jesus' *church*, which, similar to the house in the previous section, is an identity label for the community of faith. Those who have entered the new covenant, like those in Matt 7 who hear and do his words, are being built upon the rock.

Passage	Matthew 7	Matthew 16
Building	House	Church
Foundation	Rock	Rock
Threat	Storm, winds, rain	Gates of Hades
Outcome	It did not fall	The gates of Hades shall not prevail

With two references examined, a pattern is starting to be established within the book of Matthew. Jesus, and the gospel he preaches, is associated with a rock that is the foundation piece to his new covenant community. Matthew 21:42 provides a final expansion to the rock theme where Jesus directly refers to himself as the *cornerstone*. He states, "Have you never read in the Scriptures: 'The stone that the builders rejected has become the cornerstone; this was the Lord's doing, and it is marvelous in our eyes?'" Like many other stone references we will explore, this one is an OT quotation from Ps 118 which is contextually linked to the temple. This concept will be unpacked more in the Pauline literature below and in the next chapter

---

7. See Martin, *Bound for the Promised Land*, 81–86.

but what is worth immediate attention is that the text once again focuses on a *structure* that has a rock *foundation*. Matthew, for a third time, has recorded content linking Jesus to a foundational stone upon which a structure is built.

Matthew is not the only biblical author picking up on the rock motif. Other Gospel accounts incorporate some of these same references into their records. Due to the similarity of the these other accounts, a treatment of Mark, Luke, and John will be bypassed to focus upon the other NT references and allusions to the stone motif.[8]

PAUL

Paul makes numerous comparisons of Christ to the rock. In 1 Cor 3:11, he states, "For no one can lay a foundation other than that which is laid, which is Jesus Christ." Here, he goes on to describe the church of Corinth as a temple—a concept we will discuss at length in later chapters—but lying beneath this temple structure is a foundational stone. This foundation is unique in that no other foundation can be laid for this particular structure. Though the city of Corinth was inundated with temples and shrines to foreign deities which were certainly built on various high places and stone footings, the temple of YHWH was altogether different in its locale and, most importantly, its composition as Christ was the sole foundation of the edifice.[9]

Paul expands upon this rock imagery in his letter to the Ephesians where he states, "So then you are no longer strangers and aliens, but you are fellow citizens with the saints and members of the household of God, built on the foundation of the apostles and prophets, Christ Jesus himself being the cornerstone, in whom the whole structure, being joined together, grows into a holy temple in the Lord" (Eph 2:19-21). Once more, the building imagery is evoked to move the reader's imagination towards a construction project where stones are being arranged together on top of a giant foundational rock.[10] Again, the temple of God is in view as Paul describes the characteristics of its composition. By identifying Christ as the *cornerstone*,

---

8. For more on these, see Lanier and Keith, *Old Testament Conceptual Metaphors*, 168–213; Beale and Carson, *Commentary on the New Testament*, 212–14; and Hoskins, *Jesus as the Fulfillment*.

9. Fee, *First Epistle to the Corinthians*, 150–60.

10. For more on this building imagery, see Hoehner, *Ephesians*, 397–99.

The Rock: Jesus Christ

he draws the same conclusions Matthew did by quoting the OT to position Christ as the foundation of God's new covenant building.

Outside the scope of building foundations, Paul compares Jesus to rocks in other ways. In Rom 9:33, Paul describes Jesus as being a stone of stumbling and rock of offense in his quotation of Isa 8:14. Though this does not directly link the rock to a foundational element, some of the previous connections to the temple mentioned earlier are still present. Speaking of God, Isaiah states, "He will become a *sanctuary* and a stone of offense and a rock of stumbling" (italics mine). Between this reference and Isaiah's mention of Mount Zion four verses later (Isa 8:18), it is not difficult to see that Paul borrows and quotes from a theological context of temple imagery where Mount Zion serves as the foundation.[11] In doing so he continues the theme of building even though negative outcomes are the focal point. The terms *offense* and *stumbling* simply reveal the inverse effect of the building metaphor for those who reject God's foundational proposition. Rather than being *built up* on the stone, they are *broken down* by it. By emphasizing the negative aspect of the rock metaphor, Paul parallels Matthew's two-way system where one can choose to build on the rock and experience blessing or fall under the judgment of the rock. Both the positive and negative outcomes associated with the rock are consistent to the overarching theological metanarrative.[12]

First Corinthians 10 provides another reference to the rock motif where a loose connection to falling or stumbling is in view. Here, Paul recalls the Israelites' wilderness wandering where the people were thirsty and God supplied their need miraculously through a water-producing rock. Not only that, but as they wandered in the arid environment of Sinai, the rock followed them around, in one sense or another, and continued to supply enough water to hydrate the entire nation.[13] Paul's reason for bringing

---

11. Douglas Moo connects the stone of stumbling to the cornerstone motif as well. See Moo, *Letter to the Romans*, 628–30.

12. Snodgrass, *Christological Stone Testimonia*, 262–66, here refers to the positive and negative sides of the rock metaphor as the "twofold effect."

13. There are some theologians who believe Paul was referencing a commonly held rabbinical viewpoint, that the rock of Horeb, described in Exod 17:6, physically followed the Israelites during their wilderness wandering. See Enns, "Moveable Well." Others have suggested that Paul envisions the term "rock" as a metaphor for God so that it is actually YHWH following the Israelites rather than a rock. See Albright, *Yahweh and the Gods*. Still, others see Paul as embracing the rock as a manifestation of God's presence in similarity to his appearing in the burning bush, the angel of the Lord, and the incarnation of Jesus. See Thiessen, "Rock Was Christ."

this up was to remind the Corinthian church that the Israelites were not immune to temptation and compromise, even though they "drank from the spiritual Rock that followed them, and the Rock was Christ" (1 Cor 10:4). He links Jesus to the rock to remind the church that the Messiah has what they need in order to quench their spiritual thirst, but holiness is not guaranteed to the individual simply upon the basis of being present within the community of faith.[14] Holiness is separation from the world and union with Christ. Those thinking they are in union with Jesus but who are actually, in practice, united to this world are cautioned, "Take heed lest he fall" (1 Cor 10:12).

To summarize, Paul's references to Christ through stone imagery are similar to those of Matthew in that they either depict Christ's building plan or, conversely, his demolition process. He is either a rock for building up, or a wrecking ball for those who seek to build apart from him. Even in 1 Cor 10, where the discussion of "falling" is linked to Christ the rock, Paul progresses the discourse towards ecclesiological *construction* by compelling the congregation to *build up* (1 Cor 10:23). Here, the Greek word for *build* is *oikodomeō* and is the same language utilized in Eph 2:22 where the church is being *built* upon the chief cornerstone, Jesus Christ.[15] These theological connections are centralized around rock terminology and further emphasizes the need to explore the antecedent texts from which these allusions draw.

PETER

Before moving to those OT passages that undergird the NT depiction of Jesus as the rock, it is important to consider one last account. Peter, who was at the center of Jesus' church-building-rock statement in Matt 16, writes a portion of Scripture that is more potent than all the other passages so far. He states,

> As you come to him, a living *stone* rejected by men but in the sight of God chosen and precious, you yourselves like living stones are being built up as a spiritual house, to be a holy priesthood, to offer spiritual sacrifices acceptable to God through Jesus Christ. For it stands in Scripture: "Behold, I am laying in Zion a *stone*, a *cornerstone* chosen and precious, and whoever believes in him will

---

14. Fee, *First Epistle to the Corinthians*, 494–509.
15. See Akright, "Role of 'In Christ,'" 123–58.

not be put to shame." So the honor is for you who believe, but for those who do not believe, "The *stone* that the builders rejected has become the *cornerstone*," and "A *stone* of stumbling, and a *rock* of offense." They stumble because they disobey the word, as they were destined to do. (1 Pet 2:4–8; italics mine)

This pericope is an amalgamation of the numerous rock references already covered in the Gospels and Paul. Peter incorporates them collectively to show the theological progression that has transpired since Jesus' initial statements. Christ promised that he would build his church on the rock and now Peter suggests, through the use of rock terminology, that his work is well underway. And like the Gospels and Paul, there is an element of *destruction* that is embedded within the conversation of *construction*. While the cornerstone underlies Jesus' construction project, the stone may indeed be the downfall of those who reject Christ.[16]

CONCLUSION

The material above is not an exhaustive list of the NT's references to Jesus as the stone or rock. However, the content provided should instill a sense in the reader that these monikers are prevalent and that the NT has a unified witness to Jesus' identification with the *rock*. From context alone it is clear that stones were recognized for their ability to uphold structures and protect from outside threats. Yet, it seems equally obvious that these same stones could be perceived in a negative way, where an unfortunate encounter could result in injury or death. Together, these positive and negative aspects of the rock are placed in juxtaposition to one another to compel the audience to react. There appears to be an emphasis on one's relationship to the covenant embedded within the use of the rock metaphor.

Though the literary contexts surrounding these rock references provide a layer of interpretative clarity, the theological load of the rock demands that the historical context be considered as well. For thousands of years, this symbol had been used and recapitulated in the redemptive story of God's people and has come to the NT text as a centerpiece of Christology. The vast number of references to Jesus as the rock imply that the audience had a shared imaginary regarding the features of this rock but, unfortunately, the modern reader's disconnection from this social awareness diminishes the accuracy of their interpretive intuition. So, while the literary

---

16. Schreiner, *1, 2 Peter, Jude*, 110–13.

context reveals that Jesus is the foundation of the church, the security for the believer, and the judge against those who do not build on his word—i.e., the rock of offense—does it stand that the rock metaphor's historical use assumes more than these literary explications? I not only believe that it does, but am convinced that a better grasp of rock theology will shed light on the literary context within which these quotations and allusions sit.

The next chapter will begin the process of developing the doctrine of the rock. The focus will shift to the temple, a subject that serves as the basis for many of the NT quotes provided above. Though this is only one layer of the total theological load that the symbol carries, the temple aspect of the rock metaphor is not insignificant, but is central to the social imaginary of the first century audience's understanding. For those seeking to grasp the nuances of NT Christology, this layer is crucial.

2

The Rock: The Temple

IN MANY WAYS, CHRISTOLOGY is developed on the foundation of rock and stone terminology. Since both OT and NT writers employ rock language to communicate their ideals, it is a worthy endeavor to trace the connective tissue between these references to establish how they relate to, and inform, one another. The concept of *the cornerstone* is one topic within this area that is extremely significant. The NT provides numerous references to Christ as the cornerstone—and synonymous designations, like *foundation*—and these do not arise out of thin air, but are expressions derived from the Scripture of the first-century Jew.[1] The Psalms and the book of Isaiah are particularly significant in relation to these themes as numerous quotes and allusions regarding Christ can be traced back to these books as source material. Within the context of these OT antecedents, the temple arises as a premier feature and is the focal point of NT usage. The cornerstone, though associated with numerous theological realities in Jewish literature, is in the most literal sense the foundational rock upon which the temple in Zion was built.[2]

The theology of the NT demonstrates that Jesus' body is the new temple and the point of access where heaven and earth intersect.[3] These

---

1. Wright, *New Testament*, 241–43.

2. In addition to the temple foundation, the cornerstone has been associated with the nation of Israel, the community of faith, the Davidic king, and the Messiah. See Neusner, *Babylonian Talmud*, 20:250; Schreiner, *1, 2 Peter, Jude*, 108–9; Vaillancourt, "Psalm 118," 721–38.

3. Many NT books point to the fact that Jesus is the new temple but John is very explicit in his christological portrait. In John 1:51 Jesus compares himself to the "house

writers communicate this theological truth through recapitulating OT descriptions of the temple and applying them to Christ. The quotations and allusions formulating the NT's Christ-as-temple motif are centered around a cluster of OT passages, namely Isa 8:14–15, 28:16, and Ps 118:22. Interestingly enough, some of the NT writers merge two or more of these passages together as if they were quoting a single passage.[4] Romans 9:33 is one example where Isa 8:14 and 28:16 are quoted together with no hint of separation in location or context. First Peter 2:7–8 does this even more drastically as it combines Isa 8:14 and Ps 118:22, passages from separate books, into one blanket quote. If this tells us nothing else, it reveals that there is such an assumed unity of thought among NT authors regarding the rock motif in the OT that they could select and utilize rock and stone references at-will with very little concern regarding contextual abuse.[5] Looking at each of these passages within their literary, historical, and cultural context will reveal that there is indeed a unity of thought.

ISAIAH 8:14–15

> *And he will become a sanctuary and a stone of offense and a rock of stumbling to both houses of Israel, a trap and a snare to the inhabitants of Jerusalem. And many shall stumble on it. They shall fall and be broken; they shall be snared and taken.*

Isaiah 8:14–15 is not only the source material for Rom 9:33 and 1 Pet 2:7–8, but it is also referenced by Jesus in Matt 21:44, and is likely the idea lying behind texts such as 1 Cor 1:23 where Christ is presented as a "stumbling block" to the Jews. These NT authors are not proof-texting their theological arguments by snatching OT passages at random, but share common circumstances to Isaiah and the other writings they quote. Therefore, it is

---

of God" in Jacob's vision at Bethel by describing himself as the place where angels will "ascend and descend." In John 2:13–22, Jesus cleanses the temple and states, "Destroy this temple, and in three days I will raise it up." John provides a point of clarification that Jesus was talking about the temple of his body. In John 4, Jesus discusses the nature of sacred space with the woman at the well and says, "Woman, believe me, the hour is coming when neither on this mountain nor in Jerusalem will you worship the Father. . . . But the hour is coming, and is now here, when the true worshipers will worship the Father in spirit and truth, for the Father is seeking such people to worship him." See Hoskins, *Jesus as the Fulfillment*.

4. Schreiner, "Peter, the Rock," 114.

5. See Schreiner, "Peter, the Rock," 99–117.

not only the quoted verse that is of importance for interpreting these NT passages, but an understanding of the greater contextual surroundings of the OT quotation being employed.

The grammatical-historical examination of Isa 8:14–15 positions these rock images within the greater context of war, the Mosaic covenant, and the idea of divine security. The Assyrian armies and their king, Tiglath-pileser III, presented an imminent threat to Judah and all other surrounding nations during Isaiah's time. In response to this threat, alliances were formed between the Northern Kingdom (Israel) and the nations of Aram (Syria) to muster a defense.[6] Yet, they temporarily turned their aggression toward Ahaz, Judah's king, threatening war over his refusal to join the Syro-Ephraimite league. The words of 2 Kgs 16:7–9 indicate that Ahaz had a treaty of his own and it was with the very entity the Syro-Ephraimite league was trying to fend off.[7]

The prophecy of Isaiah brings a condemning accusation against Ahaz for seeking security outside of God since the Mosaic covenant emphasized that protection was to be found in YHWH, not political alliances or other forms of power.[8] In response, God sends a twofold message of judgment and deliverance which runs from Isa 7—the famous *Immanuel* passage—all the way through chapter 9. It is made clear in this section of prophecy that God would protect Judah from the immediate threat but not without judgment for seeking security outside of YHWH.

At the center of this prophetic section lies the passage under review that further reveals the two-edged nature of God's intervention. YHWH, in Isa 8:14, is depicted as both a sanctuary *and* a stumbling stone.[9] Much like the NT two-way pattern examined in the previous chapter, Isaiah begins to develop both positive and negative aspects of the rock metaphor. God's presence as *sanctuary* and *rock/stone* are both textually and conceptually tied to the temple.[10] Therefore, Isaiah can be interpreted as warning and

---

6. Smith, *Isaiah 1–39*, 199–201.
7. House, *1, 2 Kings*, 336–37.
8. Motyer, *Prophecy of Isaiah*, 82.
9. Motyer, *Prophecy of Isaiah*, 95.
10. *Sanctuary* is translated from the Hebrew *miqdas*, a word almost exclusively used in reference to God's dwelling place throughout the OT. In the exodus narrative, it referred to the tabernacle where God chose to *dwell among* the people but by the time Isaiah prophesied, *miqdas* had become synonymous with the temple. Additionally, it should be noted that Isaiah summarizes that the source of these prophecies originated from Mount Zion where the temple was built in Isa 8:18. Since both stone and rock are

comforting simultaneously through the reminder of God's temple-presence at Zion.

Though God has many warnings for various nations throughout the book of Isaiah, it is Israel who stands condemned as the one stumbling over the rock. At this point in history, the Northern Kingdom had completely abandoned the covenant of YHWH for the high places of Bethel and Dan (2 Kgs 15:28).[11] After Israel's separation from Judah under the leadership of Jeroboam I, there were political reasons for discouraging temple worship as its location required travel to the Southern Kingdom and, more importantly, Jerusalem.[12] God, however, had not changed his covenant stipulation regarding the place of sacrifice which resulted in the entire Northern Kingdom falling under condemnation of covenant unfaithfulness for neglecting God's presence on Mount Zion. Consequently, Israel is prophetically dedicated to destruction in Isa 9:8–21 and is the target of Isaiah's river metaphor in Isa 8:5–10. Here, Israel's spiritual neglect and covenantal abandonment are highlighted by the nation's preference for *northern* security over the security found in the *waters of Shiloah*—the water source of Jerusalem. In choosing the protection of a physical king over that of YHWH, Israel is breaking covenant with God and establishing a new covenant with Rezin and his pantheon of gods.[13] In a bit of irony, Israel's abandonment of Zion's river is depicted through the language of *flood judgment*. The swelling of the Euphrates river—a water source associated with the region of their "protectors"—is prophesied to sweep the Northern Kingdom away.[14] Because Israel had neglected God's temple and entered into unholy alliances, going as far as to attack God's people, they demonstrate their disconnection from the covenant community and suffer the corresponding judgment clearly articulated under the Mosaic law (Deut 30:17–18). In describing this judgment of floodwaters, the name Immanuel is employed twice (Isa 8:8 and

---

utilized alongside the portrait of God as sanctuary, and since they are also expressions of God's presence just like the sanctuary, it seems plausible to contextually view these elements as references to the temple, or at least a literary use of synecdoche where rocks and stones symbolize the entire structure.

11. Elwell, *Baker Encyclopedia of the Bible*, 1636–37.

12. Archer, *Survey of the Old Testament*, 161.

13. Oswalt, *Book of Isaiah*, 197–98. While Oswalt interprets the parties of the alliance differently than that being proposed above, his point on covenantal relationships is universally applicable to every treaty of this kind.

14. Motyer, *Prophecy of Isaiah*, 91–92.

8:10) reminding the audience that "God with us" is not always a pleasant reality but can result in divine judgment.[15]

The Northern Kingdom clearly *stumbles* over the rock of the Jerusalem temple, but Judah also fails in this area. Isaiah 1:12 records God's disgust with Judah's sacrifices where he states, "When you come to appear before me, who has required of you this trampling of my courts?" The people's total disregard for God's covenant stipulations—such as caring for the widow and the orphan—have revealed their disregard for YHWH and rendered their sacrificial offerings unacceptable. These failures, coupled with the country's alliance with Assyria, leave Judah susceptible to the judgement of God if they remain in rebellion. The floodwaters of Isa 8:5–10 do not recede before reaching the Southern Kingdom but swell to the very *necks* of its inhabitants. Yet, God mercifully becomes a sanctuary to them against the Assyrian threat, whom the waters symbolically represent. Unfortunately, Judah's ongoing rebellion and covenant violation results in their own taste of judgment with the conquest of the Babylonians in 586 BCE, where the sanctuary was desecrated and the symbol of God's presence destroyed.

The purpose of this brief historical sketch is not for biographical purposes but rather to clarify the way in which Isaiah uses the rock metaphor in relation to cultural and theological developments. Isaiah employs the language of *rock* to evoke a covenantal awareness of God's presence within the temple, and to recall the covenantal aspect of security that was clearly articulated at Sinai and again from the plains of Moab as recorded in Deuteronomy. Those walking faithfully in covenant with God, and therefore depending on him instead of forming political alliances, can take comfort in the God-with-us motif of Isaiah's prophecy. However, the use of *Immanuel,* and the variety of temple references that contextually surround the name, are not intended to comfort those outside the covenant but, rather, symbolize the devastation of divine judgment that comes on those seeking other sources of security. The storm waters will rise and destroy those who build on such a faulty foundation, yet, those established on Zion will thrive.

---

15. Some commentators interpret the unholy alliance here as that between Ahaz and Assyria rather than the Northern Kingdom and Aram. See Childs, *Isaiah*, 72–73, and Oswalt, *Book of Isaiah*, 225–26. The judgment, then, is the conquest that will come against Judah, rather than Israel. The interpretive variation has no bearing on the developments of my argument but I am in agreement with Motyer who sees the flood waters as a threat to Judah, but not a description of destruction as is the case with the Northern Kingdom. This description fits well with the Immanuel promise made in the previous chapter, and better explains how the waters of Jerusalem were abandoned. See Motyer, *Prophecy of Isaiah*, 92.

Where the NT quotes Isa 8:14–15, it is likely that the thematic elements above are still at play, even though the historical context has drastically changed. When Paul quotes the passage in Rom 9:33, he is not in a political war, nor does he envision the physical temple in Jerusalem as a sanctuary as was the case in Isaiah. However, he does view the *church* as the temple of God (1 Cor 3:16; 6:19) and is *combating* Judaizers by teaching that the covenant community excludes those who seek the wrong security—i.e., their own good works. For Paul, judgment will come upon all who are not fully united to the cornerstone of Christ. Peter's use of Isa 8 seems to follow a similar line of thought as he describes believers as a new nation, priesthood, and temple (1 Pet 2:5, 9). Being built on the cornerstone of Jesus, they reflect the holiness of God and "proclaim the excellencies" of him who called them out of darkness. Those outside this new community of priests, however, are described as a people who stumble over the rock (1 Pet 2:8).

Even where Isa 8 is not directly quoted, there are still elements of Isaiah's theological context that permeate the literary employment of the rock metaphor. Jesus' teaching of the wise man who built his house upon the rock seems to parallel the imagery of Isa 8 very closely. Those refusing to trust the words of God in Isaiah suffer the same fate as those who do not *hear* and *do* the words of Christ in Matt 7. In both cases, the chaotic waters act as the agent of judgment upon those refusing to build upon the only real security that exists—the Lord and his word. Those who hear God and do what he has commanded experience covenantal security against external threats.

ISAIAH 28:16

> *Behold, I am the one who has laid as a foundation in Zion, a stone, a tested stone, a precious cornerstone, of a sure foundation: "Whoever believes will not be in haste."*

Isaiah 28:16 is a record of prophetic utterance that continues within the same historical context of the passage above with only one likely exception—the alliance. Though Isa 8 highlights the alliance of the Northern Kingdom to Aram, and possibly Ahaz's alliance with Assyria, the context of Isa 28 seems to have an alliance with Egypt in view.[16] Regardless of who the alliance is with, the primary emphasis of the prophet is the same. Israel and Judah are guilty of leading their people away from the covenantal

---

16. Oswalt, *Book of Isaiah*, 504–20.

The Rock: The Temple

protection of YHWH and into alliances with human protectors that will not prevail.

In response to this failure, Isaiah describes the consequences with the familiar language of storm waters. Isaiah 28:2 states, "Behold, the Lord has one who is mighty and strong; like a storm of hail, a destroying tempest, like a storm of mighty, overflowing waters, he casts down to the earth with his hand." While describing the destruction of the Northern Kingdom, Isaiah turns his attention to his primary audience, Judah, who also is coming under judgement for their unholy alliance and covenantal unfaithfulness. Their alliance is described as a "covenant with death" and an "agreement with Sheol" that will topple under the judgement of YHWH. Isaiah 28:17 states, "And I will make justice the line, and righteousness the plumb line; and hail will sweep away the refuge of lies, and waters will overwhelm the shelter."

Sandwiched between the passages describing judgment of the Northern Kingdom and that of the Southern Kingdom is the double-edged rock metaphor that, once again, communicates both judgment and deliverance. The rock, here, is an explicit symbol of Zion and portrays the temple-presence of God as a structure that stands in juxtaposition to the "shelter" of Judah's political alliance. The *pinnāh* (cornerstone) is described as a "sure foundation" that is a "tested stone." It is a secure building structure for those who "believe," or in other words, "trust" in the covenantal promises of God. Rejecting these covenantal promises by procuring unholy alliances, on the other hand, has been determined to be a faulty and insecure structure according to the standard of God's plumbline of justice (Isa 28:17).

To summarize, Isa 28 builds on the rock motif established earlier in Isa 8. Both references to the rock have the temple-presence of God in view and portray Zion as bringing judgment to those who abandon YHWH for other deliverers but salvation to those trusting in his covenantal promises. These references provide literary pictures for the audience that portray two systems of faith through building imagery. Those trusting in worldly political alliances to protect against the outside threats are depicted as a structure that collapses under the storm waters. However, those who believe in the covenantal promises of YHWH bind themselves to the only building that will withstand such threats—the temple in Zion. It is being argued here that these prevailing themes are borrowed and recapitulated in the teaching ministry of Christ as he describes the new community of faith. He is building a structure—i.e., his church—upon a rock—i.e., his gospel—and reminds his audience that those building on any other structure are like fools who build on the sand where storms destroy and kill.

PSALM 118:22

> *The stone that the builders rejected has become the cornerstone.*

Having looked at Isaiah's portrait of the rock motif, we now turn to the way the Psalter utilizes the rock metaphor. As with many of the Psalms, there is a certain degree of ambiguity regarding the authorship and circumstances surrounding its composition. Nevertheless, Ps 118 has been highly regarded by Jews and Christians alike. In Judaism, this passage was, and is still, used during the Passover celebration at the conclusion of the Seder meal. It has been suggested by some that David wrote this Psalm while returning to his throne after being temporarily displaced by his son, Absalom.[17] The depiction of divine deliverance and military victory found throughout the chapter justify such an interpretation. Furthermore, Ps 118:19–20 could describe David's ascent and reentrance into his kingdom where it states, "Open to me the gates of righteousness, that I may enter through them and give thanks to the Lord. This is the gate of the Lord; the righteous shall enter through it." Regardless of whether or not these assertions are factual, it is clear that the chapter describes God's deliverance in juxtaposition to those who trusted in man's power. It is also clear that a procession towards the temple is being described, which likely became the precedent for the Psalm's Passover connection as the pilgrimage would require a similar ascent for most travelers.[18]

For the Christian, the importance of Ps 118 can be understood in the various ways the theology of the chapter is applied to Christ in the NT. Not only is the relationship between Christ and the cornerstone utilized by NT writers to depict the salvific nature of Jesus' arrival, but it also emphasizes his temple status. Regarding salvation, the psalmist walks the reader through the various trials that he has suffered and endured. Though he was oppressed by human enemies, God preserved the psalmist and became his

---

17. See Guenter, "Blessed Is He Who Comes," 425–47.

18. The passage describes the processional reaching the "gates of righteousness," a blessing pronounced from "the house of the Lord," and the response "bind the festal sacrifice with cords upon the horns of the altar," all of which restrict this portrait to a temple event. See Longman, *Psalms*, 854–45.

salvation (Ps 118:14). In verse 21, the psalmist repeats the refrain "he has become my salvation" and proceeds to explain *how* in the cornerstone passage. That which was rejected—presumably the psalmist who was driven out of Jerusalem—has been reinstated by God. Salvation, here, is portrayed in a similar way to that of Isaiah's cornerstone usage. The one who did not trust in the power of "man" or "princes" has experienced the covenantal protection of YHWH.

Even though the cornerstone reference in Ps 118 seems to be focused more on a person than a building, the metaphor being employed cannot be disconnected from the temple. The idea of a structure, as in Isa 8 and 28, still resonates within the literary portrait being crafted. There are *gates* for entrance, a *cornerstone* for foundational stability, and a reference to the *house* of the Lord—a place where sacrifices occur on the altar (Ps 118:27). Whatever the circumstances are behind this chapter, it clearly portrays a restoration project through the language of the building metaphor. Furthermore, the psalmist depicts two groups of people who mirror the two-way pattern seen in Isaiah. There are those who *rejected* the cornerstone (Ps 118:22), and those who celebrate the rock's inclusion into the structure of the building—"it is marvelous in our eyes" (Ps 118:23). Those trusting in the covenantal promises of God over the security of worldly power find salvation in Zion and witness God's restorative building program in action.

CONCLUSION

Isaiah 8:14–15, 28:16, and Ps 118:22 are not the only places the stone motif arises in the OT in connection with Zion. Space limitations do not permit a full examination of the related passages here, but these three sections do provide a look at the most significant points of interaction between the NT portrait of Christ and the OT portrait of the temple. By quoting and alluding to these temple portraits, the NT presents Jesus as a recapitulation of the OT temple and the ancillary benefits that accompanied those who trusted in the God indwelled therein. Like the cornerstone of Zion, Jesus is the object of salvation and provides the believer with protection from death or Sheol. Jesus in the NT, much like YHWH in the OT, is engaged in a building program that utilizes a rejected cornerstone as its foundation (Matt 21:42–44; Eph 2:19–22; 1 Pet 2:4–5). Those connected to these salvation stones are immune to the chaotic storm waters that symbolically represent the powers of death. Yet, both Testaments divide humanity among the two-path categories and condemn those who are not connected to the covenantal rock building. These "rejectors" will be crushed under the weight of the power of this rock.

3

The Rock: The Mountain of God

THE PREVIOUS CHAPTER EXPLORED the temple as one of the assumed points of continuity between the OT and NT's use of the rock motif. Of great importance were the *cornerstone* passages which, in their original setting, tied the rock testimonia of the OT to the foundation of God's house in Jerusalem. While these references seem to employ a building metaphor in which a particular stone is chosen as the foundational corner piece, there is another foundation of the temple that should be considered in relation to these cornerstone references. The mountain chosen by God for the placement of the temple—i.e., Zion—has both a biblical and traditional identity as the cornerstone and arises in Scripture, both logically and chronologically, prior to the building stone discussed in the previous chapter. This chapter will explore the mountain of God as a forerunner to the cornerstone motif.

THE MOUNTAIN OF GOD: ZION

A brief historical sketch will help create a proper orientation towards the hermeneutic being proposed. To begin, the temple did not come to the Israelites as an act of human ingenuity, but rather as a direct designation from God. Long before David's request to build God a house, YHWH had already commanded, "But you shall seek the place that the Lord your God will choose out of all your tribes to put his name and make his habitation there. There you shall go, and there you shall bring your burnt offerings and your sacrifices, your tithes and the contribution that you present, your vow offerings, your freewill offerings, and the firstborn of your herd and of your flock" (Deut 12:5–6). Only YHWH had the authority to designate the place of divine habitation. Any effort to manipulate his presence through temple construction outside of this designation would have been staunchly rejected, as YHWH refused to be served in the likeness of the foreign deities of Canaan.[1]

This is of great importance as it demands that we recognize the placement of the temple as a designated sacred space, chosen by God. Furthermore, this passage suggests that God made his name to dwell in Jerusalem logically—if not chronologically—prior to the actual building of the temple. In fact, God's designation of Zion as the dwelling place for his name is the *cause* of the temple's construction. Any other cause would be a violation of Deuteronomy's prescription. This *cause* is further reflected in Solomon's prayer of dedication where he describes God's house as *"the place of which you have said, 'My name shall be there,'* that you may listen to the prayer that your servant offers *toward this place"* (1 Kgs 8:27–30; italics mine). Though the biblical narrative never provides a direct reference within which God commands the Israelites to build a temple in Jerusalem, Solomon's language echoes the command of God in Deuteronomy and provides reasonable evidence that an unrecorded conversation included this important designation.

As the biblical record unfolds, the designation of Jerusalem becomes more certain within the Prophets, Psalms, and historical Writings, where these accounts reflect the prevailing issue of unauthorized altars and high places among God's people (e.g., 1 Kgs 3:2–3; 13:32; 2 Chr 28:22–27; Ps 78:56–72; Ezek 43:7). The division of Israel from Judah resulted in numerous worship sites that were not divinely sanctioned and, thus, were inadequate for accessing YHWH. As these writers recorded and reflected upon this sinful abandonment of the covenant, they employed the image of *Zion* in juxtaposition to the unauthorized sites as a call to repentance (Ps 97:7–8; Isa 2:1–22; 10:10–12; 57:13; Jer 8:19; Mic 1:1–16). The temple mount became a symbol of God's covenant blessing and was used as both an encouragement to the righteous and a warning to the rebel that YHWH would uphold the stipulations of their Sinai agreement, for better or worse.

With this historical setting in mind, it is likely that the descriptions of the cornerstone as a rejected stone, a stumbling stone, and a crushing stone are literary responses towards the Northern Kingdom's disdain for Jerusalem

---

1. Woods, *Deuteronomy*, 186–88.

The Rock: The Mountain of God

as a worship site. Their self-appointed "high places" had become substitutions for the location God had designated for divine access and communion. However, it was not just the temple precinct that was rejected by those of the north, but the entire mountain upon which it stood. Jesus' conversation with the Samaritan woman in John 4 highlights this lingering contempt for Zion where the woman states, "Our fathers worshiped on *this mountain*, but you say that *in Jerusalem* is the *place* where people ought to worship" (John 4:20; italics mine). The Samaritans were descendants of the Northern Kingdom's tribes, and the woman's words reflected a long-held religious belief system of this lineage.[2] The most significant point of her statement is that she rejected the *mountain* of Jerusalem, not just the temple, as a sacred worship spot. While Jesus detaches the point of divine access from any mountain as a mark of the new covenant, he does provide a brief rebuke in saying, "You worship what you do not know; we worship what we know, for salvation is from the Jews" (John 4:22). In other words, Jesus recognizes Jerusalem as the revealed point of divine access under the old covenant and links it to the *salvation* of God. The Samaritans, on the other hand, historically rejected the cornerstone for rocks that could not save.

The literature of the Qumran community provides a complementary look at how certain segments of Israel contemporary to the NT era viewed Jerusalem as a part of the rock motif.[3] In document 4Q522, the Prophecy of Joshua, the writer states, "For behold a son is born to Jesse, son of Perez, son of Ju[dah]. . . . [He is to take] the Rock of Zion and from there he is to possess the Amorites . . . to build a house for the Lord, the God of Israel" (4Q522 9 II, 2–5).[4] This translation of the fragment envisions a future Davidic conquest that fulfills the occupation of Canaan and drives the enemies out of Jerusalem. While the details of when and how this will take place are unimportant to the topic at hand, what is significant is the designation of Jerusalem as the "Rock of Zion."[5] This reference not only distinguishes the

---

2. Potts, "Samaritans," 1436.

3. It should be noted that the blanket phrase "Qumran community" does not necessarily describe a homogenous group of people, but more than likely diverse group sects. However, there are certain ideas that permeate the majority of literature indicating that certain beliefs existed as unifying thread among those represented by this moniker.

4. This translation is taken from Vermes, *Complete Dead Sea Scrolls*.

5. There is a possibility that the reference "Rock of Zion" is referring to the "son born to Jesse." However, it could be strictly speaking of Jerusalem or even both subjects simultaneously. Chapter 5 will deal with how some biblical references capture both the king and the temple in the rock metaphor, and it is likely that sources building off these theological portraits are doing the same.

mountain as a rock, but establishes it as the place where God will set up his kingdom, temple, and priesthood.[6] Though the document is written from the perspective that these ideas had not yet materialized, the mountain of Jerusalem is clearly delineated as the locale for these anticipated realities and stands as a rock of significance in the minds of the Qumran community, despite their negative opinion of the current state of affairs.

The greatest reason for viewing the mountain of Zion as a part of the OT's rock testimonia is the biblical record itself. Isaiah 30:29 states, "You shall have a song as in the night when a holy feast is kept, and gladness of heart, as when one sets out to the sound of the flute to go to the mountain of the Lord, to the Rock of Israel." This passage is written as a form of Hebrew poetry and incorporates the element of *parallelism* to describe the salvation God brings to his people. By placing "mountain of the Lord" next to "Rock of Israel," a literary equivalence is established and a metaphorical exchange takes place.[7] Isaiah, here, employs a common artistic literary device to describe Israel's mountain, Jerusalem, as God's rock.

In summary, the mountain of Jerusalem is theologically connected to the rock motif of Scripture. Not only was it the physical rock bed upon which the temple was erected, but was also a sacred space designated by God logically and chronologically prior to the temple's construction. The mountain represented the stability and provision described within the stipulations of the Mosaic covenant and became widely associated with YHWH's salvation. Furthermore, those who rejected this mountain as the divine access point stumbled over this rock inviting judgment from the God who had made his name to dwell in Zion.[8] Therefore, this mountain

---

6. The document goes on to describe the building of the temple and the establishment of a priest figure who will serve in the temple while the people dwell eternally in security (4Q522 9 II, 6–9a).

7. See Berlin, *Dynamics of Biblical Parallelism*, 31–32; 99–103.

8. It should be highlighted that the context of Isa 30:29 shares many of the same contextual elements of Isaiah's cornerstone texts and the NT's borrowing of those texts. Here in Isa 30, the mountain of God is the place of security while those outside of God's divine protection experience "his breath . . . like an overflowing stream that reaches up to the neck" (Isa 30:28). The violent description of the chapter portrays YHWH reaching down from the mountain of the Lord and bringing devastation with "storm" and "hailstones." Isaiah 8, 28, and Matthew's rock references discussed in the previous chapters, each portray the rock as salvation from the chaotic waters of judgment. Isaiah 30 does not depart from that rock-based theme. Additionally, it joins these other portions of Scripture in presenting the rock as dual natured: a blessing for those faithful to the covenant, and a curse of judgment for those who reject.

became the ruin of many countries and peoples who failed to recognize it as the intersection of heaven and earth.

THE MOUNTAIN OF GOD: SINAI

Before Jerusalem was designated as the mountain of the Lord, Mount Sinai would have naturally assumed that designation in the Jewish mind. God appeared to Moses there multiple times, once during the burning bush encounter and again following the exodus from Egypt. The initial meeting between God and Moses was at Mount Horeb, an alternative name for Sinai, where YHWH revealed his intentions, his name, and the sacredness of the mountainous location in one conversation. It was here that God required Moses to remove his sandals because he was standing on "holy ground" (Exod 3:5). He would go on to require that the Israelites return to "this mountain" to *serve* him (Exod 3:12).

The focus on *serving* is crucial for seeing the connection between Sinai, the evolving temple system, and its apex at Zion. God's words to Moses in Exod 3 echo throughout the OT where *serving* becomes a metric for measuring faithfulness (Deut 8:19; 10:12, 20; 28:47–48, Josh 22:25; 24:16–31; Judg 2:11–13; Ps 100:2). An example can be seen in Exod 23:24–25, where God provides a warning to the Israelites regarding their relationship to foreigners, stating, "You shall not bow down to their gods nor *serve* them, nor do as they do, but you shall utterly overthrow them and break their pillars in pieces. You shall *serve* the Lord your God, and he will bless your bread and your water, and I will take sickness away from among you" (italics mine). Furthermore, the word *serve* (*awbad*) is regularly employed within the context of the priesthood and temple/tabernacle worship.[9] Therefore, God's encounter with Moses invites the Israelites to leave their bondage and enter a form of priestly service at Sinai. It is upon this rock—the mountain of God—that YHWH establishes the Israelites as a "kingdom of priests" and a "holy nation" (Exod 19:6). Sinai's connection to this priestly *service* establishes an early template upon which the theology surrounding Jerusalem is constructed later on in the biblical narrative.[10]

Another text that highlights Sinai's foreshadowing of Zion is the song of Moses following the Red Sea deliverance. In Exod 15:17, Moses concludes his song with these words, "You will bring them in and plant them

---

9. Beale, "Eden, the Temple," 7–8.
10. Levenson, *Sinai and Zion*, 91–92, 187–88.

on your own mountain, the *place,* O Lord, which *you have made for your abode, the sanctuary,* O Lord, which *your hands* have established" (italics mine). Before Moses had even received the Decalogue at Sinai, he was already aware that God was designating a mountain top as a sanctuary and it would come about as the work of his hands, not mans.[11] While the temple was certainly constructed by human hands, the mountain on which it came to rest was crafted by God alone.

The Rock at Rephidim

Above, it has been argued that Sinai served as the seedbed for the rock imagery surrounding Zion. As the place of origin for both the priesthood and tabernacle, Sinai provides the theological blueprint for the permanent temple and, as an earlier manifestation of the mountain of God, becomes a pivotal feature of the rock metaphor. Yet, there are additional ways in which Sinai finds its way into the theologically loaded rock testimonia. Another important association is the account of God's provision of water from a rock near Rephidim in the book of Exodus. Prior to the establishment of the Mosaic covenant, a water shortage prompted many to declare that YHWH had brought them into the wilderness to die (Exod 14:11). The people threatened to stone Moses and return to Egypt, which drives the prophet to petition God for a resolution. God's provision arises out of this predicament where he states, "Behold, I will stand before you there on *the rock at Horeb*, and you shall strike *the rock*, and water shall come out of it, and the people will drink" (Exod 17:6; italics mine).

There is considerable debate among scholars as to what this rock was, especially considering the complexity of Paul's statement in 1 Cor 10:4 where he describes this water source as a rock that "followed" the Israelites through the wilderness.[12] Still, it seems that at a bare minimum, a theological interpretation of the passage connects the rock with Sinai. The rock is designated as "the rock at Horeb," a direct reference to the place where God met Moses during the burning bush encounter. Additionally, the use of the definite article—*the* rock—indicates that this was not a random landmark, but rather a particular formation that would have been recognized by Moses.

One objection to linking this water-providing rock to Mount Sinai is the simple distinction between the Hebrew words *tsur* (rock) and *har*

---

11. Sarna, *Exodus*, 81–82.
12. Enns, "Moveable Well," 23–38.

The Rock: The Mountain of God

(mountain).[13] In most cases, *tsur* signifies a smaller rock or boulder while *har* refers to a large projectile of the earth potentially containing the mass of hundreds of boulders.[14] Yet, the author of Exodus does not refrain from using both *tsur* and *har* in similar ways to describe the location of God's presence. Exodus 17:6 employs the Hebrew word *tsur* to describe the rock at Rephidim as a platform on which God is *standing*. In comparison, Mount Sinai also serves as a standing platform where God tells Moses, "Behold, there is a place by me where you shall stand on the rock" (Exod 33:21). The same Hebrew word *tsur* is once again used to describe the rock upon which God is *standing*, even though the location is clearly the top of Mount Sinai. Though it is possible that Exod 33:21 refers to a particular rock on top of the mountain, rather than the mountain itself, the theological connection between the two is unavoidable and it is not improbable to consider that these rocks are one and the same. Furthermore, it could be that the rock of Rephidim was a formation at the base of Sinai while the rock of Exod 33:21 was at the pinnacle of the mountain. Interestingly enough, the holiness of the mountain did not just coincide with the summit but encompassed the entire structure as can be seen in the prohibition against touching the mountain in Exod 19:12. Therefore, both rocks are spatially and theologically connected by the larger mountainous structure which has been entirely designated as God's *standing* space.

Any theological discussion of the *rock* that ignores the significance of Sinai misses a wealth of historical and spiritual insight that would have been assumed among the Jewish audience of Jesus' world. Sinai was not only an important location in the history of Israel's priesthood and tabernacle, but was the location where God made himself known to his covenantal people. It was the place of their salvation, where they were liberated to *serve* their deliverer. Furthermore, Sinai emerged as a rock of protection and provision within the biblical narrative. When the people were thirsty and faced the death of drought, God brought forth the water of salvation from the least likely of places: a rock. Not only did this rock *provide*, but it later *protected* as Moses was hid in its cleft during an intimate encounter with God's holiness. The rock that preserved the life of the Israelites was now the source

---

13. See Domeris, "God, Our Rock," 24, for a look at how the various Hebrew words are used in the OT.

14. Flavius Josephus writes, "This rock is there at this day, as the travelers agree, and must be the same that was there in the days of Moses, as being too large to be brought thither by our modern carriages," demonstrating the magnitude of the rock in Exod 17. Josephus and Whiston, *Works of Josephus*, 17.

of opportunity to communion with God that had not been known since Eden. These associations to the rock of Sinai are but a few of the aspects of the stone testimonia that come to bear fruit when the NT writers utilize the rock metaphor to describe Jesus and his church.

THE MOUNTAIN OF GOD: EDEN

Israel was not completely unique in its pattern of accessing God on mountain tops. The people of the ancient Near East (hereafter ANE) regularly erected temples, shrines, and altars atop elevations they perceived to be connected to the heavenly realm.[15] In some instances, it was their superstitious view of lightning that was interpreted as a place where the gods descended to earth. Elijah's confrontation with the prophets of Baal is exemplary of this idea where *fire from heaven* was perceived as evidence that the divine realm had chosen an authorized altar (1 Kgs 18:20–40). Yet, Israel was not permitted to erect worship sites based on lightning strikes like their ANE counterparts, but instead needed direct revelation from God to establish an area for divine access. So while Israel had common elements between their sacred sites and the ANE people, there were drastic differences that set them apart. Still, the commonalities suggest an origin of mountain top worship from which these practices initially emerged.

Numerous theologians have recognized Eden as the original temple and prototype for all future temples within Scripture, including the eschatological temple in the Latter Prophets.[16] Many of these scholars have also deduced from the variety of biblical references to Eden, that a mountain existed near the garden and was the designated sacred space within which God's unique presence dwelt, a precursor to the Holy of Holies.[17] Though the Genesis account does not specifically mention a mountain near the garden, there are at least a few good reasons for this assumption. First, Gen 2:10–14 describes a river flowing "out of Eden" which would have naturally originated at a higher elevation. This image becomes more pronounced in the description of the eschatological temple in Ezekiel, where the water

---

15. Hearson, *Go Now to Shiloh*, 20–21.

16. Alexander, *From Eden*, 20–60; Beale, *Temple and the Church's Mission*, 72–76; Lioy, "Garden of Eden," 25–57; and Smith, *House of the Lord*, 35–64.

17. G. K. Beale has argued persuasively that the original creation had three distinct areas matching the tripartite division of the temple. Beale, *Temple and the Church's Mission*, 74.

The Rock: The Mountain of God

flows from beneath the temple, down Mount Zion, and becomes a source of life for creation (Ezek 47:1–12). Furthermore, the new Jerusalem in Rev 22:1–2 describes the final temple and depicts "the river of the water of life" that yields an Edenic "tree of life."[18] Furthermore, this river flows from the "throne of God" and is exemplary of a thematic pattern where water descends from God's elevated sanctuary into his creation.

Second, the various covenants recorded in Scripture are almost exclusively linked to mountain top encounters with God. The Davidic covenant was established on Mount Zion, the Mosaic covenant at Sinai, and the Noahic covenant at Mount Ararat. Even the new covenant in Christ was officially "cut" at the time of Jesus' crucifixion in Jerusalem.[19] Therefore, viewing Eden as a mountain where God's presence dwelt and where he established the initial covenant of the dominion mandate fits the biblical pattern.

The third reason for viewing Eden as a mountain comes from Ezekiel's prophetic rebuke of the king of Tyre. The passage states, "You were in Eden, the garden of God. . . . You were an anointed guardian cherub. I placed you; you were on the holy mountain of God; in the midst of the stones of fire you walked" (Ezek 28:13–14). Though there is considerable debate as to whether or not Ezekiel, here, intends to reveal an ancient account of the devil or to simply denounce Tyre's king, the point of significance for our purposes is that the prophet uses *Eden* as the setting and describes it as "the holy mountain of God." Whether Ezekiel roots this description in the historicity of the account of Satan's fall, or simply uses Edenic imagery to make a point, the language depicting a holy mountain of God in Eden could not be clearer.

Eden, therefore, is the original mountain of God and becomes a symbol, among many, of the anticipatory longing of God's people for restoration. Following Adam's sin, mankind was expelled from the presence of God, suffered the hardships of the curse, and failed to commune with the creator in any consistent and dependable way.[20] Even the people of Shinar in Gen 11 wrestled with these shortcomings as they tried to manipulate the presence of God through the erection of the tower of Babel. It was not until

---

18. While Rev 21:22 reveals that there is no physical temple in the city, the fact that entire new creation is the dwelling place of God and has many of the same traits associated with the biblical temple—e.g., the precious stones associated with the temple and the priestly garments—reveals that the entire world has been transformed into an arboreal sanctuary, similar to Eden. See Alexander, *From Eden*.

19. Gentry and Wellum, *God's Kingdom through God's Covenants*, 207–38.

20. Hearson, *Go Now to Shiloh*, 6.

God's covenant with Abraham that we began to see a reversal of the curse. From the moment mankind fell, *returning to Eden* became a central thrust of the biblical record. The tabernacle and temple symbolized giant strides in this restoration paradigm as these structures recreated Eden-like access to the creator. It is no coincidence that these sanctuaries were replete with Edenic ornamentation, reminding the worshiper of where they came from and where they were striving to return.[21] The lampstand resembled the tree of life that was placed in the middle of Eden. The precious stones within the priestly breastpiece and scattered throughout the temple furnishings were reminders of the Edenic sanctuary where an assortment of precious stones were first documented (Gen 2:11–12). Additionally, the cherubim on the veil between the holy place and the most holy place served as an ever-present reminder of the angelic guardians placed outside the garden of Eden following mankind's expulsion.[22]

Since the biblical record is so inundated with imagery harkening back to Eden, it is likely that the locations of Sinai and Zion also reflect this primordial temple in their contribution to the restoration paradigm. When Moses encounters God at Sinai, the reader should have a hermeneutical siren going off that associates the event with the *first* mountain of God. The inaccessibility to God's presence on Sinai (Exod 19:12) was a mere reflection of humanity's prohibition from reentering Eden after the fall (Gen 3:22–24). This restricted access is also echoed in the limitations associated with the Most Holy Place within the tabernacle (Exod 26:33; Lev 16:2). However, as the theme of restoration progresses in the narrative, God permits Moses access to the mountain and moves the needle of restoration even further in the creation of the priesthood. While no one was permitted back into Eden after the fall, the access of Moses on the mountain and the priests within the tabernacle provide a glimpse of movement towards restoration. Likewise, as students of Scripture read through the record of the Davidic covenant and the construction of Solomon's temple, the parallels between Zion, Sinai, and Eden emerge as another step towards this end.[23] The Israelites, at the time of the Davidic covenant, are experiencing prosperity in their own land and have God's presence in a permanent establishment at the top of the mountain. The reflection of Eden in this era of Israel

---

21. Hays, *Temple and the Tabernacle*, 22–25.
22. Hays, *Temple and the Tabernacle*, 22–25, 111–22.
23. Bartholomew, *Where Mortals Dwell*, 79–80.

The Rock: The Mountain of God

is unlike anything that had come before and is the reason why Mount Zion becomes the epicenter of theological expression.

THE ROCK IN CREATION AND CHAOS

These biblical and theological arguments are provided to demonstrate that the stone testimonia of the OT includes the various manifestations of the Mountain of God presented above, and thereby carries theological nuances into the NT's recapitulation of the rock motif. There is evidence to suggest that many of these connections were already common aspects of Jewish thought in the time period of, and leading up to, the NT writings. The Babylonian Talmud provides several rabbinic outlooks on the relationship between Mount Zion and the creation of the world. It states, "Our Mishnah-teaching accords with him who has said, 'Out of Zion the world was created'" (b. Yoma 5:2, II.1.C). The document proceeds to record an inciteful commentary on the creation account of Job 38:6 where Rabbi Nappaha states, "A stone did the Holy One, blessed be he, toss into the ocean, from which the world was founded: 'Whereupon were the foundations thereof fastened, or who laid the cornerstone thereof'" (b. Yoma 5:2, II.1.G).[24] One final comment in this section of the Talmud is attributed to "the sages" and interprets Ps 50:1–2 as a description of creation that originates out of Zion (b. Yoma 5:2, II.1.H).

A much later writing, the *Midrash Tanchuma*, reveals a similar interpretation of Ps 50:1–2, stating, "The Land of Israel sits at the center of the world; Jerusalem is in the center of the Land of Israel; the sanctuary is in the center of Jerusalem; the Temple building is in the center of the sanctuary; the ark is in the center of the Temple building; and the foundation stone, out of which the world was founded, is before the Temple building."[25] Though some of these statements were made later than the NT era, they serve the purpose of showing the continuity of thought among Jewish thinkers who viewed the cornerstone as God's mountain and central component of the creation narrative.

A cursory glance at these responses may fail to prompt a reconstruction of the creation account within our mental bank of presuppositions, but when these rabbinical testimonies are considered alongside the biblical

---

24. Translations of b. are credited to Neusner, *Babylonian Talmud*, 5:200–201.

25. Nataf, "Midrash Tanchuma, Kedoshim 10." The English translation above was borrowed from the collection at sefaria.org.

Rock Doctrine

and theological contours already explored above, it is difficult to dismiss the conclusions that many Hebrew scholars have already embraced—that the cornerstone motif began at creation. There, God created the world by throwing Mount Zion, or the cornerstone, into the watery chaos of Gen 1:2, thus plugging the waters and bringing forth life.[26] Though the designation of this cornerstone as "Zion" is anachronistically applied to the creation account, it is the mountain within Eden that is being identified with this theologically charged label. Moving forward, every reference of the cornerstone—and most theological rock references in general—describe an object that brings order in place of chaos, and life in place of lifelessness. These associations emerge into eschatological expressions where seas are absent—due to the cornerstone plugging the chaotic waters—and rivers flow to provide life for all (Ezek 47:1–12; Rev 21:1; 22:1–2).

It is from this perspective that the NT employs the rock testimonia alongside the living-water metaphor as it describes the significance of Jesus' arrival. Jesus is both the cornerstone, and the living water of life. He is the rock upon which one can build for protection against the chaotic storm waters, and he miraculously calms the storm to demonstrate the significance of this theological claim. In other words, many of the features that were expected among the Jewish adherents regarding the eschatological temple are at least linguistically associated with Jesus in the NT.

Probably the most impressive portrait of this rock-water recapitulation is seen in Matt 21 during Jesus' conflict with the religious elite of Jerusalem. Jesus has already condemned the current temple practices stating, "It is written, 'My house shall be called a house of prayer,' but you make it a den of robbers" (Matt 21:13). Returning to the city sometime shortly after, Jesus cursed a fig tree that represented the fruitlessness of the temple system. Furthermore, the withering of the fig tree was symbolically pointing to the destruction that was coming upon those who were tethered to the polluted temple practices.[27] Following these events, Jesus speaks against those defending the status quo in Jerusalem by issuing a parable suggesting the vineyard would be taken away from the current inhabitants and given to others, a likely foreshadowing of gentile entry into the Kingdom of God. He then quotes the cornerstone passage of Ps 118 which isolates the chief priests and Pharisees as *rejectors* of the stone. The narrative continues in

---

26. See, Levenson, *Sinai and Zion*, 133–35; Pula, "Rethinking the Community as Temple," 100–105; and McGlynn, "Authority and Sacred Space," 119–20.

27. See France, *Gospel of Matthew*, 791–94.

the next chapter with a parable that describes the *burning* of a wicked city. These chain of events coalesce in the portrait of Jerusalem's destruction that Jesus predicts in Matt 24. In the middle of this rock- and temple-ladened context is a passage that recapitulates the summarized metanarrative above. "Truly, I say to you, if you have faith and do not doubt, you will not only do what has been done to the fig tree, but even if you say to this mountain, 'Be taken up and thrown into the sea,' it will happen" (Matt 21:21). Jesus' language runs akin to the familiar imagery of the mountain being throne into the sea to plug the chaos and bring forth life. Those hearing these words would have likely connected the imagery with creation and the eschatological associations articulated throughout the OT stone testimonia. Since the current leaders had rejected the stone, it is they who are stumbling over the stone of the new creation. They, themselves, are the recipients of chaos, death, and destruction that Jesus predicts, since they have not built upon the cornerstone. However, the disciples who listen to Christ's words and build upon the rock will experience the order associated with Eden, Sinai, and Zion.

CONCLUSION

At the risk of being redundant, the following will summarize how the Bible's restoration paradigm progresses alongside of, and in conjunction with, the cornerstone aspect of the rock metaphor based on the comparisons made above. God plugged the watery chaos in Gen 1:2 with a mountain that will later become identified as the cornerstone. This mountain in Eden was God's earthly dwelling place and served as the origination point of all creation. From the mountain, God caused the previously chaotic waters to flow in a life-sustaining, orderly way to provide nourishment for all creation. Following an unspecified time in paradise, sin entered the world and the chaotic waters that were subdued under the cornerstone were released back into the world creating Noah's flood (Gen 7:11).

Later at Sinai, God progressed the narrative by standing on a rock from which water sprung. This miraculous provision was reminiscent of the waters flowing down from the mountain of God in Eden, which in both cases served as a life source without which the people would perish. Shortly thereafter, God stood on the rock of Sinai with Moses and provided the Israelite's with the metaphorical waters of the law.[28] Here, God hides

---

28. Scripture and rabbinical tradition connect Torah with the metaphor of water.

Moses in the cleft of the rock so that he can see a partial glimpse of God's glory. Similarly, the people of Israel would gain a partial form of restoration through the creation of the priesthood and the tabernacle system. From the rock of Sinai, the priesthood was created and authenticated as a mediatorial institution for restoring the communion of God and humanity that was last witnessed in Eden. Furthermore, the visual representation of Eden within the priestly apparel and the tabernacle furnishings reminded the people that a return to Eden was in motion.[29]

The Israelites eventually entered the promised land where they experienced many aspects of Eden's restoration including a geographical boundary within which to carry out the purposes of God and access to the presence of YHWH at a permanent sacred site, Mount Zion. Though sin results in an exile during the Babylonian captivity—similar to Adam and Eve's removal from Eden—God reveals a time of full restoration when an eschatological temple will be rebuilt upon the cornerstone.

Though these connections are not often communicated in modern contexts, the sampling of Jewish literature alluded to above indicates that these ideas were present during the NT era. The words of Jesus, the Revelator, and other biblical writers, make use of the imagery that has been formulated above and shed light on numerous passages that appeal to the relationship between rocks, mountains, and water. The progression of restoration is carried by these images and make the stone testimonia a central feature of Jesus' work, as he brings restoration to its fullest expression. The next chapter will explore the source of the rock metaphor and will reshape the chronological path of this book. Following chapter 4, the trajectory of thought will be developed chronologically forward as it builds towards Christ's fulfillment.

Consider Pss 1:1–3, 42:1, and Isa 55:1–3. Additionally the Babylonian Talmud records an interpretation of Prov 11:25, "and he who waters shall water again too," by Rabbi Sheshet stating, "Whoever teaches Torah in this world will have the merit of teaching it in the world to come" (b. Sanh. 11:1, I.30.A).

29. Where I describe a "return to Eden," I am not as much focused upon the physical location of Eden as I am the state of being that existed in Edenic paradise. It is the recovery of God's presence among his people that is being restored; however, this is spatially experienced and will result in physical placement regardless of the historical alignment with Eden's geographical parameters. See Bartholomew, *Where Mortals Dwell*, 58–59.

4

The Rock: God

Up to this point, the rock motif has been examined in its relationship to the numerous locations and objects that have been presented as theologically significant by Scripture, all of which were physical by nature. The temple was a *physical* structure, the foundation of the temple was composed of *physical* materials, and the mountains upon which God's presence was experienced were, likewise, *physical* settings within the created world. This chapter will now move the conversation from the physical domain to the spiritual, revealing how these otherwise mundane objects received their sacred identity.

GOD AS ROCK IN SCRIPTURE

Early in the biblical narrative, the writers of Scripture utilized numerous metaphors to refer to God. He was depicted as a judge (Gen 18:25), a shepherd (Gen 48:15), a father (Deut 32:6), a consuming fire (Deut 4:24), and a birth parent (Deut 32:18) to name a few examples. Among these metaphors lies one that becomes a predominant concept within Jewish thought and the ongoing revelation of divine Scripture—God as the rock. One of the first texts using rock imagery to refer to God was Moses' statement in Deut 32:4 where he declares, "The Rock, his work is perfect, for all his ways are justice.[1] A God of faithfulness and without iniquity, just and upright is he."

---

1. Genesis 49:24 may be the only earlier text where God is referred to as a rock, though the statement "stone of Israel" here is likely being applied to the "mighty one of Jacob." In hindsight it is easy to conclude that this statement is a messianic reference, and

Rock Doctrine

In this same chapter, God is described four additional times as the rock (Deut 32:15, 18, 30, and 31).

The idea of God being a rock becomes more concentrated later on in the biblical record. Hannah is one of the next individuals recorded using this description for YHWH. In her famous prayer, she states, "There is none holy like the Lord: for there is none besides you; there is no rock like our God" (1 Sam 2:2). Shortly hereafter, David ascends to the throne and repeatedly vocalizes his dependance upon God through the use of rock metaphors. David's song of deliverance in 2 Sam 22 employs the term *rock* as a synonym for God a combination of five times, with one additional reference immediately following in 2 Sam 23:3.[2] David's contributions to the Psalter are heavy with references to God as the rock. Psalm 19:14 states, "Let the words of my mouth and the meditation of my heart be acceptable in your sight, O Lord, my rock and my redeemer." David continues to speak like this in Ps 31:2–3, "Incline your ear to me; rescue me speedily! Be a rock of refuge for me, a strong fortress to save me! For you are my rock and my fortress; and for your name's sake you lead me and guide me." This pattern continues to reemerge throughout the psalter with over twenty direct references to God as the rock (e.g., Pss 18:2, 31, 46; 28:1; 42:9; 62:2, 6). The significance of this pattern becomes even more emphatic when one begins to count the *indirect* correlations between God and rock in the Psalms. Strong towers, fortresses, and other objects of refuge are tethered to the literary and conceptual fabric of the rock metaphor.[3]

By the time the prophetic books were being penned, the stone metaphor had shifted in its application to include numerous referents. Isaiah, for example, connects the metaphor to the temple, the mountain of God, and the Messiah. Still, there are a few examples where these authors attest

---

is for trinitarians, a description of God incarnate.

2. The Hebrew word *tsur* is the primary word underlying the English word rock in this passage; however, 2 Sam 22:2b uses *sela* where it states, "The LORD is my rock." There does not appear to be any distinction in meaning between the two Hebrew words but are likely a result of artistic variation. See Domeris, "God, Our Rock," 24.

3. Many of these indirect references (towers, refuges, etc.) occur within the immediate context of those passages using rock terminology to describe God. Often they occur together as complimentary ideas within the literary arrangement of parallelism. Even when these expressions occur independent of the rock metaphor, they frequently communicate the same ideas of God that are being expressed when the metaphor is present. The close association between rocks, towers, and refuges in the Psalms suggest that they exist within a linguistic family of terms that is linked conceptually rather than etymologically.

The Rock: God

to the ongoing tradition of considering God the rock. Isa 17:10 employs the phrase "the Rock of your refuge," while Isa 26:4 testifies that "the LORD God is an everlasting rock." Even God himself is recorded in Isa 44:8 posing the question, "Is there a God besides me? There is no Rock; I know not any." Habakkuk is the only other prophet directly employing the word rock (*tsur*) to refer to God. He writes, "Are you not from everlasting, O Lord my God, my Holy One? We shall not die. O Lord, you have ordained them as a judgment, and you, O Rock, have established them for reproof" (Hab 1:12).

GOD AS ROCK IN EXTRABIBLICAL LITERATURE

The Bible's testimony alone is enough to demonstrate the theological connection between the rock and YHWH within Judaism. However, there are numerous extrabiblical writings that also reveal the historicity of this relationship. The Qumran community's writings are abundant in references to the divine rock.[4] Scroll 4Q377 records the interaction between the Israelites and God at Sinai, stating, "on earth he stood on the mountain to teach us that there is no God apart from him, and no Rock like him," (4Q377 2 II, 8).[5] In another section of the scrolls, the Words of the Luminaries, the author writes, "For we too have [we]aried /God/ by our iniquities, we have tried the Rock with [our] si[n]," (4Q504 V, 18b-19).[6] While some of these references are direct quotations from the OT—e.g., the quotation of Ps 18:2 in document 4Q381—many are the community's own creative expressions for God.

Rabbinic literature also parallels the Qumran tradition of incorporating passages and biblical interpretations into their writings that use the term *rock* synonymously with God's name. In a discussion on prayer, the Babylonian Talmud records the following statement from Rabbi Abba Benjamin: "And the word 'rock' refers only to the Holy One, blessed be he, as it is said, 'Of the rock that begot you you were not mindful' (Deut. 32:18)" (b. Ber. 1:1, III.19.E).[7] In tractate Menahot, a rabbinic discourse is initiated surrounding the meaning of the rock metaphor, stating, "*R. Judah Nesiah asked R. Ammi, 'What is the meaning of the verse of Scripture*, "Trust in the

---

4. For example, 1QpHab V, 1; 1QS XI, 4; 1QHa XVII, 28; 1QHa XIX, 18; 4Q254 7:3; and 4Q381 24:7.

5. Martínez and Tigchelaar, *Dead Sea Scrolls*, 745.

6. Martínez and Tigchelaar, *Dead Sea Scrolls*, 1017.

7. Neusner, *Babylonian Talmud*, 1:27.

Lord forever, for in Yah, the Lord, is an everlasting rock'" (Is. 26:4)?" (b. Menah. 3:7, II.7.C).[8] The rabbis represented in this text suggest that the rock metaphor depicts a refuge for the God-fearer in both this life and the life to come.

SIGNIFICANCE OF THE GOD-AS-ROCK REFERENCES

The examples provided indicate that the rock metaphor stood as a representation of God in the Jewish mind from the time of Moses well into the NT era. However, these examples do not clearly demonstrate exactly what was being communicated about God through the use of figurative language. Metaphors often convey meaning in ways that are not entirely predictable or clear. For instance, when God is compared to a rock, what features or aspects of stone should the reader naturally apply to God? Should they assume that God is strong because rocks are observably durable? Is God to be regarded as eternal since grass, trees, and all other life withers away in death while rocks tarry generation after generation? There are numerous possibilities of comparison that would uphold clearly revealed attributes of God. Yet, there are also comparisons that could be made which would fall outside orthodoxy. Rocks are not omnipresent, they have no emotion or will, their physical integrity can be compromised under certain conditions, etc. These are but a few characteristics of rocks that would be ignored when the metaphor is employed. But the question remains, which characteristics of God are highlighted by the rock testimonia?

The quick and easy answer to this question is to remind the reader that context drives meaning. As one interprets each passage comparing God to the rock, the surrounding content will be essential for deciphering the meaning of those texts. A cursory glance at the biblical references, as well as the supplementary rabbinic and Qumran statements, will reveal that the metaphor is intended to convey different meanings in its various usages. David's use of the God-rock metaphor in 2 Sam 22 compares the military protection of rock fortresses, strongholds, and refuges to God's divine protection within David's military conquests. In contrast, Moses' reference to God as the Rock in Deut 32 is more ambiguous and is contextually linked to YHWH's justice, faithfulness, and perfection. So, while the rock metaphor cannot be oversimplified to univocally limit the interpretation to a

---

8. Neusner, *Babylonian Talmud*, 19:171.

The Rock: God

single attribute of God, most of the references fall into one or more of the following categories.[9]

The first category within which rock references contextually fall into are those revealing God's ability to *protect* and *preserve*. Davidic authorship is responsible for the vast number of these references as his military conquests required divine protection and provision for victory. His escape from the hands of king Saul, his defeat of the Philistine armies, and his return to the throne following Absalom's rebellion are but a few examples of the triumphs David credited to divine intervention. While not every military victory is specifically preserved in rock references, the way David uses the metaphor in his liturgy looks back on a long history of preservation and speaks to the general protection offered by YHWH.[10]

A second way the OT contextually uses the rock metaphor is as a symbol of *steadfastness*. Expressions, like Hab 1:12, demonstrate that the rock metaphor represents God's ability to establish his people in a way that is firm and unyielding. There is great overlap between this category and the previous one as steadfastness is dependent upon protection and preservation, yet the idea of steadfastness is broader than the first category in that it reaches beyond militaristic circumstances. The rock metaphor's portrayal of divine steadfastness is expressed in descriptions of God's perfection and righteousness, both of which emphasize his eternal and unchanging nature (Deut 32:4; Isa 26:4; Hab 1:12). Furthermore, the eternality and immutability of God is presented as a basis, or reason, for why his people should faithfully commit their lives to him. Isaiah 26:4 states, "Trust in the Lord forever," with the command's basis being "for the Lord God is an everlasting rock." Not only is God's steadfastness in view when the rock metaphor is employed, but also the steadfastness imparted to believers which enables them to resist falling into sin and unbelief (Ps 40:2).[11]

A third category of symbolism regarding the rock is that of *provision*. The overlap is, once again, obvious as God's protection often assumes any number of provisions in the process. However, the OT's use of rock imagery is often employed as a specific expression of God's ability to provide. In Gen 22, Abraham obeys God's command to sacrifice Isaac upon Mount Moriah but amidst the process, God interrupts and provides a sacrificial

---

9. For a thorough discussion of how analogical language can reveal attributes of the infinite, see Freeman, "Church's One Foundation," 132–41.

10. Goldingay, *Psalm*, 257–58.

11. Goldingay, *Psalms*, 570.

substitution. This mountain is later revealed to be the site of the temple in 2 Chr 3:1, meaning that Moriah was theologically, if not historically, linked to Jerusalem. Therefore, the future *mountain of God* where the temple will be located—and thus, the cornerstone—derives its significance from this earlier occasion. Abraham's name for the location, *YHWH Yireh* (the LORD will provide), tethers *divine provision* to the stone testimonia.

Shortly after this in the biblical record, God's provision is connected to the rock where he miraculously provides water from a rock at Mount Horeb. This event becomes the source material for numerous OT passages that highlight God's ability to provide (Ps 105:41; 114:8, Isa 48:21).[12] Psalm 78:20 serves as one example where it states, "He struck the rock so that water gushed out and streams overflowed. Can he also give bread or provide meat for his people?" This rhetorical question assumes an affirmative answer and emphasizes God's provision through the recapitulation of the rock of Rephidim.

Another category is the rock metaphor's association with God's *salvation*. YHWH is a rock because he has provided salvation to his people. Salvation, however, should not be oversimplified to the confines of only one particular understanding of the term. Though Christians often view salvation through the particular lens of spiritual renewal and eternal life, the OT's portrait of God's salvation is multifaceted and often specifically circumstantial. Returning to David's employment of the rock metaphor in the Psalms, Israel's king recognizes his military conquests as a form of God's salvation (Ps 18:2; 62:2).

Additionally, there are references to the salvation of the rock that are connected to God's *creation* or *origination* of a person or group of people. The early reference to God as rock in Deut 32:15 states, "But Jeshurun grew fat, and kicked; you grew fat, stout, and sleek; then he forsook God who made him and scoffed at the Rock of his salvation." The passage draws a parallel connection between the phrase "God who made him" and "Rock of his salvation," indicating a link between the rock metaphor and God's fatherhood of the people of Israel. Psalm 89:26 leads us further to this conclusion where it uses the phrase "Rock of salvation" alongside a description of God as "Father." Though the context here describes the relationship between YHWH and Israel's king rather than the nation of Israel, the idea that God made the king—i.e., gave him his authority—is understood as a *saving*

---

12. See Domeris, "God, Our Rock," 22, where he speculates that this event could be the source of the God-as-rock metaphor.

The Rock: God

act. Isaiah 51:1–2 also draws a parallel between the rock-as-salvation and the idea of *formation*, though in this context it is arguably Abraham who is the rock. Still, behind Abraham's *fatherhood* of the nation is the covenantal blessing of God that is responsible for prospering Israel.

The final category—though this is by no means an exhaustive list—is the simple representation of God's presence and holiness through the rock metaphor. Not only do certain uses of the rock metaphor represent the abiding presence of YHWH, but they resemble his glorious presence in contrast to the mundane world. Throughout the OT account, there are numerous references to gold, silver, onyx, jasper, diamond, and a variety of other jewels. The first appearance of these precious stones occurs in the Gen 2 account of Eden, where gold, bdellium, and onyx are listed. Ezekiel 28:13 also provides a description of Eden and lists nine unique gemstones in addition to gold. A similar combination of gemstones was used in the composition of the priests' breastpiece for their service in the tabernacle (Exod 28:15–30). Gold, silver, and precious stones were also among the materials David collected for the building of the temple in 1 Chr 29:2.

In all of these occurrences, the stones represent the holiness of God and his presence. Eden was the place where God walked with humanity in perfection and holiness, until they sinned and were kicked out. The priesthood served in the task of mediating the divine presence and were responsible for entering the tabernacle to offer sacrifices for the sins of Israel. When the people saw the priestly vestments, they would have been reminded of the ultimate goal of restoration; to reenter Edenic holiness and bliss. The temple was the house of God, and the stones would have reminded them of the original house of God in Eden. They would have also been reminded of the loss that was wrought through sin. The precious stones would have impressed upon the community the need for holiness. As a rare gem stands out from among the ordinary rocks of the world, so does God stand apart from the creation as one infinitely valuable and worthy.

NT authors undoubtedly worked from these categorical presuppositions as they employed rock terminology in their own writings. The category of protection, salvation, and steadfastness are seen in Jesus' teaching on the two houses (Matt 7:24–27). The house upon the rock provides security from the storm, leading to salvation. The steadfastness is clearly depicted in the outcome, where the house on the rock is left standing whereas the house on the sand has fallen. The rock metaphor in Matt 16:16–19 draws from these same categories as the church is protected from the gates of hades. They are steadfast upon the cornerstone of salvation. Paul's recapitulation of the rock of Rephidim reveals that Jesus was the rock that followed the Israelites around in the wilderness and provided them with life-sustaining water. While the exact interpretation of this event is debatable, the idea that Christ was, and is, the *provision* his people needed is not. In the concluding chapters, we will look more closely at the implications for NT interpretation of the rock motif, but these examples suffice to demonstrate the potency of these categories.

DIVINE "MIRRORING" IN THE ROCK METAPHOR

Arguments have now been made that link the stone testimonia of Scripture to, not only God, but also the temple, its foundation, and the mountain upon which it stood. How then, did a Jewish community, which recognized the holiness of God as completely distinct and transcendentally different from the creation, tether these physical elements into the same identifying language as God the creator?[13] Does the shared identity indicate some form of equality between YHWH and the temple, or does the metaphor speak uniquely to each referent irrespective of the others? The progression of the biblical narrative seems to indicate that these physical components inherit their share in the rock identity as a result of God's designation of sacred space and the convergence of his presence with these holy areas. In other words, the temple, the cornerstone, Zion, and the other manifestations of *the mountain of God*, are not *the rock* in and of themselves but receive this identity label as a result of God's designated presence at these sites. Without the presence of God, these locations cease to share in the identity recapitulated in the sacred rock paradigm.

There are numerous reasons for drawing these conclusions. The first being that the rock testimonia never excludes God at any moment. YHWH is the rock at the beginning of the OT record, and he retains that identity throughout the biblical corpus. His rock identity continues to surface in the Qumran writings, the Talmud, the Pseudepigrapha, the literature of the Patristic Fathers, and is regularly expressed in Christian liturgy today.

Second, the places associated with God's presence—i.e., *sacred spaces*—change as God moves. We've already tracked the progression of the rock from Eden to Jerusalem, noting the geographical shifts of these

---

13. For a thorough treatment of holiness as a distinct aspect of God's nature, see Otto, *Idea of the Holy*.

sacred sites in response to God's relocation. However, a significant point to highlight is that these *former* sacred sites do not retain their uniqueness after God has moved on.[14] Once Zion is established as the capital, no one is recorded seeking the safety and security of Sinai. In fact, the OT reveals the error of returning to these former sites with any expectation of salvation; the reason being that God is no longer there to provide that salvation. He alone—not physical stones or mountains—is the rock of salvation.

By way of example, God revealed himself to Jacob in Gen 28 at a place that is renamed Bethel, the *house of God*. The reason Jacob renamed the area is because God had revealed in a dream that there was a convergence between heaven and earth at that particular location. The angels ascending and descending on the stairway led Jacob to believe that Bethel was a point of access to the Creator, and this location becomes a significant point of divine communion on multiple occasions moving forward (Gen 31:13; 35:1–15; Judg 21:2). A rock is then set up as a symbol of God's presence.[15] However, sometime after divine access was established at the Jerusalem temple, the Northern Kingdom returned to this former sacred site as a substitute for Zion. If this site was holy in the past and offered access to God, there was a logical expectation among the northern tribes that he might be approached in Bethel once more. Unfortunately, this notion ignored God's imperative to worship *only* where he had made his name to dwell. The prophets, therefore, bring forth an indictment of idolatry against Israel for abandoning the presence of God at Zion and *multiplying transgression* in Bethel (Jer 48:13; Hos 10:15; Amos 4:4). Consequently, the stone and altar of Bethel had become no more theologically significant than the rocks of Nebraska.

A third component of the identity-sharing that occurs between God and the other objects of the rock metaphor can be better understood through an examination of what theologians call *communicable attributes*. While there are certainly attributes of God that belong to him and only him, there are some attributes of God that are, in the words of Charles Hodge, "positive, relative, transitive, and communicable."[16] These are attributes that God shares with the created order, permitting objects and

---

14. See Hearson, *Go Now to Shiloh*.

15. Freeman, *Church's One Foundation*, 78–79. Here, Freeman draws many valuable insights from the Bethel record. He explains that it was the stone itself, not the city, that received the direct label as the house of God and, therefore, serves as an early example of how God and stone converge in the biblical record.

16. Hodge, *Systematic Theology*, 375.

beings to mirror certain divine qualities.[17] When Jerusalem is described as the "holy mountain of God," this reveals nothing special about the mass of dirt, rock, and mineral deposits lying beneath Judah's capital but, rather, reveals something about the God who uses Zion to reflect aspects of his nature. Similarly, God's designation of the Sabbath as a holy day (Exod 20:11) reveals nothing innate concerning the seventh day itself, but recognizes a corresponding value between this particular day and the activity of God. Holiness, likewise, is mirrored by places and things who exist as a reflective vessel of God, who alone is holy (Rev 15:4).[18] Outside of the communicable attributes that are shared with creation, nothing is holy, eternal, or sacred. And while every part of creation mirrors the creator to some extent, it is this special and unique mirroring of God's holiness that is on exhibition in the rock metaphor. Through mirroring particular qualities associated with YHWH's holiness, the objects of the rock metaphor are transformed into significant features of the restoration storyline.

CONCLUSION

The Bible frequently employs the rock metaphor to refer to God. It is through these images that the reader can draw conclusions by comparing the invisible Creator with his visible creation. However, a lack of knowledge about God or the object he is metaphorically compared to can lead the reader to misunderstand the intended purpose of the figure of speech. Furthermore, the context of the metaphor provides significant cues as to what the author intended to convey through these symbolic expressions. God is a lot of things, but not every metaphor seeks to exhaust the totality of his attributes at each point of comparison. Additionally, the various iterations of the rock metaphor should not be interpreted as congruent expressions. In other words, when God is compared to a rock in three different contexts, it should not be assumed that each instance employs the entire gamut of the metaphor's theological load, nor should each of the three references be forced into an identical interpretation. Every iteration is unique to its context, yet patterns do emerge within which this family of metaphors can be grouped categorically.

---

17. See, Grudem, *Systematic Theology*, 202–3, for a look at "holiness" as a communicable attribute of God.

18. Otto, *Idea of the Holy*, 25–30.

The Rock: God

When God is compared to a rock, he is often depicted as protector, provider, creator, savior, and as one who is steadfast and holy. These categories not only reveal truths concerning God's nature, but they also provide clarity on how other objects take on the rock identity. To the extent that people, places, and things mirror the various attributes of God, they also mirror the divine nature and thus receive labels that are teleologically aimed at the Creator. Yet, God has bestowed upon his creation remarkable opportunities to participate in the exaltation of his name, and has utilized various places to reveal his glory. In the next chapter, we will move from the *places* that have reflected the attributes of God, and thus received the designation of the *rock*, and look at the *people* who are separated out under the use of the rock metaphor.

5

The Rock: The King

THE PREVIOUS CHAPTERS HAVE demonstrated the wide array of purposes the stone testimonia has served in advancing the biblical narrative and the various theological developments that contribute to this advancement. The *vehicle* of the metaphor—i.e., the rock—has been employed alongside a variety of subjects, each carrying a unique contribution within the collective stone testimonia of Scripture. The last chapter provided the connective tissue for these distinct aspects of the metaphor by revealing God as the unifying thread of this biblical tapestry. The interconnectivity between God and the other aspects of the metaphor collaboratively reveal a progressive storyline to the careful reader. Though humanity experienced a loss of *divine presence* under the curse, the stone testimonia portrays a reversal of this loss as God breaks into history to reunite with his people. Sacred spaces, like Bethel, Sinai, Zion, and the temple, each communicate this progression of God's restoration. This chapter will further expand the restoration motif by examining the king of Israel as the rock, or more specifically, the cornerstone.

RESTORATION THROUGH KINGSHIP

For approximately four hundred years, Israel operated without a human king under a theocratic form of government.[1] Under this arrangement,

---

1. This date assumes that the giving of the law on Sinai was the beginning of this political arrangement. The four hundred year time frame assumes an early dating of the exodus event, which is debatable. See Elwell, *Baker Encyclopedia of the Bible*, 737.

The Rock: The King

God ruled over the people utilizing judges and prophets to reveal his will for the nation. The divine presence was not experienced in the intimate way it was in the garden of Eden, yet communion with God increased through tabernacle access and prophetic instruction. The sacrifices received at the tabernacle were the Israelite's way of reaching out to God and the prophetic utterances were YHWH's words to his people. Despite the positive movements within the theocratic arrangement, the people were ultimately dissatisfied and their preference for a human king materialized into the Jewish monarchy. While this transition was certainly a rejection of God (1 Sam 10:19), the idea of human regency was not inherently evil. The *dominion mandate* in Gen 1:26 was God's own appointment of a human ruler to represent his sovereign reign on earth.[2] Following the curse, a promise was made to Adam and Eve, and then reiterated in various ways to Abraham, Jacob, and their descendants, that a messianic ruler would one day arise from the race of man to restore the brokenness of the fall.[3] Therefore, desiring the fulfillment of these messianic expectations was not evil in and of itself. It was the motive behind this transition—"that we also may be like all the nations"—that brings the indictment against Israel regarding their political desire (1 Sam 8:20).

God's accommodation of this transition from theocracy to monarchy is further evidence that the idea of human regency was not diametrically opposed to the plan of restoration. In retrospect, NT readers can see that most Jewish kings fail to advance the restoration paradigm in any significant way, but simultaneously recognize that Christ's ministry fulfills many of the molds created by the OT monarchy. Therefore, God takes the sinful ideas of humanity and transforms them into a mechanism for accomplishing divine prerogatives.

Within the monarchy, restoration language arises in the form of the stone testimonia, linking the monarchy to the person and presence of God. While each king was supposed to represent God's rule by adhering to, and enforcing, the covenant, it was David above all else who served as the standard-bearer of the monarchs.[4] David is known, not only as a righteous king, but also as an inspired author of numerous Psalms. Furthermore, his contributions to Scripture provide some of the most colorful portraits of

---

2. Barrett and Carson, *Canon, Covenant, and Christology*, 50–51.

3. For a thorough treatment of this theme see, Kaiser Jr, *The Promise-Plan of God*., and Dempster, *Dominion and Dynasty*.

4. House, *1, 2 Kings*, 323.

the stone testimonia available. It is of no coincidence that the Bible's development of the cornerstone becomes a symbol of the Davidic covenant.

THE KING AS CORNERSTONE

The direct associations of David to the rock are far less abundant than those describing God, but there are two references that have historically been interpreted as Davidic. The *cornerstone* passages of Ps 118:22 and Zech 10:3–4, each have ties to the house of David and tether the king to the restoration of the temple. Psalm 118:22 has already been discussed in previous chapters as a direct reference to the temple, and will receive further treatment here to justify how the rock can represent both the temple and David simultaneously. The discussion will then move to Zechariah's cornerstone reference to examine how the rock metaphor evolves from king to eschatological messiah.

The question that must first be addressed before a Davidic interpretation of Ps 118:22 can be rationalized is, *how can a single passage's reference to the cornerstone be interpreted as the temple and David simultaneously?* A brief answer to this question lies at the heart of one of the main purposes for this book; to demonstrate the progression of revelation. It is the progressive nature of Scripture that permits a hermeneutical shift in meaning as the narrative unfolds. I am not suggesting that Scripture changes its meaning over time, but rather, the intentions of the writing become more clear with each passing stage of God's revelation.

A quick example of the phenomenon lies in the virgin birth narrative of the NT. While the Matthean account undoubtedly depicts Mary as a virgin who had never known a man sexually prior to the birth of Jesus, it does so on the basis of a text from the OT. However, the OT passage quoted by Matthew comes from Isa 7:14, which in its original context, would have been interpreted as a prophecy unfolding in Isaiah's time. The prophecy of a *virgin* giving birth was a sign *for* king Ahaz and would be of no effect if only fulfilled hundreds of years later at the time of the nativity.[5] Since the Hebrew *almah* can mean either *virgin* or *a young girl of marriageable age*, it is likely that the sign is fulfilled by the latter option, and her pregnancy is a result of procreation, not miraculous conception.[6] This interpretation is even more compelling when one considers the definite article preceding

---

5. Oswalt, *Book of Isaiah*, 209–12.
6. See Motyer, *The Prophecy of Isaiah*, 84–85.

the reference—i.e., *the* virgin—a likely indication that a particular female from their day was in view.[7] However, the LXX translates *almah* using the Greek equivalent *parthenos*, which narrows the semantic range to *virgin*. Since Matthew employs *parthenos* rather than a more ambiguous term, he demonstrates that the original prophecy had the potential to be fulfilled in various ways. Therefore, it is likely that Isa 7:14 had an immediate interpretation for Ahaz and other contemporaries, but also possessed enough ambiguous material for God to employ in later stages of revelation. This shift does not insinuate that Scripture changed over time, but that the clarity of God's intended meaning was intensified as more information became available. The way Jesus described the entire OT as pointing to him (Luke 24:27), even though specific christological interpretations were hidden from the original audience, indicates that this is how Scripture was designed to operate.[8]

Returning to Ps 118:22, it is common to find a variety of opinions regarding the identity of the cornerstone. Some scholars prefer a Davidic identity while others believe the reference to be linked to the Jerusalem temple, not to mention numerous other alternatives to these prominent viewpoints.[9] It is likely, however, that multiple interpretations are justified, especially in light of the unifying connection to the God–as–rock motif established in the previous chapter. If God's presence is the basis for inclusion in this motif, then a dual interpretation of the cornerstone is justified since both the temple and king were recipients of the divine presence.[10] Moreover, the king's rule involved oversight of the temple and the priesthood. Even though the king was not a priest, could not offer sacrifices, and had limitations of accessibility within the sanctuary, his proximity to the tabernacle

---

7. Childs, *Isaiah*, 66.

8. It is not my intention to suggest that *all* Scripture has "dual meaning,"—though in cases like Isa 7:14 this may be true—but to recognize that the clarity of revelation is enhanced with each successive layer that God provides in the biblical testimony. Even where prophecy seems to speak to immediate circumstances that are later employed in a christological sense, it should not be assumed that the prophet had two ideas in mind at the time of his utterance or while crafting the written record. God's pattern of recapitulating historical events in ways that are increasingly significant to the biblical storyline is a primary explanation as to how these allusions and quotations are employed in new ways, despite the real significance of their original occurrence.

9. See Vaillancourt, "Psalm 118 and the Eschatological Son of David," 722–23.

10. Not only is the king referred to in the Scripture as God's "son," (Ps 2:7; 72:1; 89:20–26), but he also possessed a special anointing of God's Spirit that was not commonly present among men (1 Sam 16:13, Ps 51:11).

and his duties as the shepherd of Israel connected him to the sacred service of mediating God's presence. The king's responsibilities overlapped with the priests' to such an extent that many texts use language blending the throne and temple (e.g., 2 Chr 2:12, Ps 2:6–7, and Isa 18:7). The close association of the king and the priesthood has led one Hebrew scholar to state, "creation, kingship, and temple thus form an indissoluble triad."[11]

In addition to the king and the temple sharing points of commonality in their representation of the divine presence, the unfolding of messianic content through revelation invites an *expandable interpretation* of the cornerstone, similar to the treatment of Isa 7:14 above. Though Ps 118:22 may have *initially* been interpreted as a reference to the temple, the progression of revelation experienced in the prophetic writings resulted in a greater emphasis on messianic interpretation, which may have given birth to the Davidic emphasis. A defense for this hermeneutical shift can be seen in the way that Ps 118 is applied to Christ who is depicted as not only the Davidic king, but also as the temple of God.[12]

If Isa 7:14 can have an immediate context with an interpretation that differs significantly from the later christological fulfillment of the text, credulity should not be assumed on the part of those who expect similar fulfillment and hermeneutical clarity regarding the cornerstone passages. Psalm 118 is notably connected to the temple in the way it employs terms related to the sacrificial system (Ps 118:27) and the physical structure of God's house—e.g., gates, stones, builders, house, and altar. Yet, Scripture and Jewish tradition link Ps 118 with the lineage of David. It is this exact chapter that is rehearsed by the Israelites on Palm Sunday as Jesus made his way to the temple. As people laid clothes and palm branches before Christ, they declared, "Hosanna to the *Son of David*! Blessed is he who comes in the name of the Lord! Hosanna in the highest!" (Matt 21:9 *italics mine*). Did these bystanders quote Ps 118:25–26 because Jesus was the royal son of David, or was it because he was entering Jerusalem to cleanse the temple? Likely, it was both. The prophetic anticipation had built concerning the Davidic heir who would restore, not only the monarchy, but the temple of God.[13] Now, through the process of progressive revelation, it had become

---

11. Levenson, *Zion and Sinai*, 109.

12. For a development of both ideas together, see Barber, "Jesus as the Davidic Temple Builder," 939–43.

13. I have written extensively elsewhere on the idea that Jesus fulfills the anticipation of a Davidic temple builder in his formation of the church. For a more in depth look at this concept, see Crawford, *Where Has Sacred Space Gone?*, 87–123.

The Rock: The King

more plausible in hindsight to recognize both institutions as antecedents of the cornerstone passage.

Looking further into Matt 21 provides even more clarity on the union of the king and temple in relationship to the cornerstone. Jesus enters the temple in Matt 21:12 and rebukes the entire enterprise as a consequence of the practices that had emerged. He declares the place to be a "den of thieves," turns over tables, and drives out the money changers. He then curses the fig tree, an act many scholars interpret as a foreshadowing of the ruin to come upon the temple and the nation.[14] When one looks ahead to the prediction of Jerusalem's destruction in Matt 24, it is clear that these ideas are materializing within the narrative. Matthew 21, then, captures the disgust among the Pharisees and other religious elites over Jesus' drastic, and seemingly *unauthorized* actions within the temple (Matt 21:23). Jesus responds with the parable of the tenants, where he borrows from Isa 5 to relay that the failures of Israel's past are being repeated in the present. This dialogue comes to a climax in Jesus' quotation of Ps 118:22, where he self-identifies as the cornerstone and indicts the Pharisees for rejecting him. He goes on further to declare that the "*kingdom* of God will be taken away from you and given to a people producing its fruits" (Matt 21:43 *italics mine*). An interpretive question naturally arises for the reader as they process this rebuke's relationship to the cornerstone reference. *Is it the Pharisees' rejection of Jesus, the Davidic king, or Jesus, the temple reformer, that is responsible for this condemnation?* The context of Matt 21 seems to imply that both topics are tethered together in Jesus' mind, and Matthew's audience would have been familiar with the nuances of the cornerstone that pertain to both subjects. One cannot separate the messianic reign from temple restoration, since any temple system that did not come under the authority of God's Messiah would have been a pseudo-sanctuary and deviation from his revealed plan.

Regardless of how the cornerstone passage of Ps 118:22 was initially interpreted, it seems evident that the revelation of NT Scripture brings clarity to an otherwise ambiguous text. The various interpretations of the cornerstone find a unifying figure in Jesus, who is both the Davidic monarch and the true temple of God. There is still, however, another reference to the cornerstone to consider that will also shed light on these conclusions. This final reference comes from the prophet Zechariah who writes during the post-exilic period

---

14. See France, *The Gospel of* Matthew, 791–94; and Telford, *The Barren Temple and the Withered Tree.*

to encourage the Jews in their rebuilding efforts. Within this book is a focus upon, both, the restored monarchy and the restored temple.

In Zech 10:3–4, it states, "My anger is hot against the shepherds, and I will punish the leaders; for the Lord of hosts cares for his flock, the house of Judah, and will make them like his majestic steed in battle. From him shall come the cornerstone, from him the tent peg, from him the battle bow, from him every ruler—all of them together." In this portion of Zechariah, the prophet depicts a day of restoration that comes for the house of Judah. Alongside the cornerstone reference are two symbols—the tent peg and the battle bow—as well as an allusion to the perpetual rule of the house of Judah. The tent peg already carries Davidic connotations from the imagery of Isa 22:22—25, where Eliakim is described as the tent peg wielding the "key of David."[15] Additionally, the idea of a perpetual rulership is also an obvious link to the Davidic covenant. David was the one promised a perpetual dynasty that would never fail to have a king on the throne (2 Sam 7:12–16). The *battle bow* is the most ambiguous reference, but still invites a Davidic interpretation since David was one of the most triumphant warriors in the OT storyline. Not only did he slay Goliath, a host of Philistines, and win numerous battles against those inside, and outside, of Israel, he writes extensively about his battles in his contributions to the psalter (e.g., Pss 3, 7, and 18). Additionally, God refused to allow David to build the temple as a consequence of the immense bloodshed associated with his reign (1 Chr 22:8).[16] Naturally, the caricature of the king stands at the helm of any royal description associated with battle, such as the "battle bow" mentioned here, thereby inviting a Davidic interpretation.

These connections are made even more clear in the context of Zechariah, who frequently references the "house of David." He draws from previous writings, or at least oral tradition, in promising that "the Branch" will come to restore Judah.[17] Of great interest to our topic is that the *Branch* is responsible for bringing restoration to both the throne and the temple. Zech 6:12–13 states, "Thus says the Lord of hosts, 'Behold, the man whose name is the Branch: for he shall branch out from his place, and he shall build the temple of the Lord. It is he who shall build the temple of the Lord and shall bear royal honor, and shall sit and rule on his throne. And there shall be a priest on his throne, and the counsel of peace shall be between

---

15. Klein, *Zechariah*, 294–95.
16. Thompson, *1, 2 Chronicles*, 165.
17. Elwell, *Baker Encyclopedia of the Bible*, 376–77.

them both.'" Once more it must be acknowledged that there was likely an initial interpretation of this text that identified the Branch with figures like Zerubbabel, who as descendants of the Davidic line, took up significant roles in the rebuilding of the Jewish nation.[18] However, hindsight allows us to look back at these texts and see with greater clarity the corresponding elements to which the later revelation testifies and, in doing so, draw differing conclusions from those who first received the prophetic utterance.

More will be said about the christological interpretations associated with these texts in chapter seven but, for now, the point of significance is that both the monarchy and the temple were united in the prophetic utterances of Zechariah, who employs the rock metaphor to establish his theological ideas and advance the unfolding metanarrative of the stone testimonia. Likewise, Ps 118:22 also brings these two elements together into union. The cornerstone, in both passages, carries the weight of the temple and the king and brings these implications to bear in their NT context. It should be briefly mentioned that the word for cornerstone in Ps 118:22 is slightly different than the word employed in Zech 10:4, the latter deriving from the Hebrew *Pinnah* (cornerstone) and the former from *Rosh Pinnah* (head of the corner). While some have chosen to make much ado regarding these differences, the NT seems to have no problem applying both terms to Christ in the same context without explanation or a sudden shift in ideas (1 Pet 2:6–7).[19] The rock, whether head stone or cornerstone, stands as a physical piece of the structure without which the entire edifice would fall.

THE KING AS ESCHATOLOGICAL TEMPLE-BUILDER

The convergence of the monarchy and the temple within the language of the stone testimonia provides a certain contour to the messianic expectations observed in the NT and contemporary literature. DSS document 4Q522, a Prophecy of Joshua, was quoted in chapter 3 and describes a Davidic king who is expected to establish a tent of meeting in Jerusalem at the end of time. The passage also conveys that the king would drive away the Amorites and Canaanites in order to fulfill this eschatological expectation for the *rock of Zion*. While the phrase *rock of Zion* contextually points—at least in some

---

18. The name Zerubbabel literally means "shoot of Babylon" and seems to be the implied figure based on word choice. See Elwell, *Baker Encyclopedia of the Bible*, 377.

19. For a preview of those arguing for a distinction, see Cahill, "Not a Cornerstone!" 345–57.

English translations—to the location of Jerusalem, there appears to be a unity between the sacred space associated with the tent and the royal figure who will physically drive out the enemies to usher in temple restoration.[20]

Document 4Q174 speaks specifically to the eschatological temple reconstruction that will happen under the headship of the *Branch*. The document is a midrash on 1 Sam 7:10–11a and states, "This 'place' is the house that [they shall build for Him] in the Last Days, as it is written in the book of [Moses: 'A temple of] the Lord are you to prepare with your hands; the Lord will reign forever and ever'" (4Q174 III, 2–3).[21] It goes on to explain, "This passage refers to the Shoot of David, who is to arise with the Interpreter of the Law, and who will [arise] in Zi[on in the La]st Days, as it is written, 'And I shall raise up the booth of David that is fallen' (Amos 9:11). This passage describes the fallen Branch of David, [w]hom He shall raise up to deliver Israel" (4Q174 III, 11–13).[22] These samples of Qumran literature demonstrate that this sectarian community associated the rebuilding of the temple with a Davidic figure who would fulfill the messianic predictions of the OT.

The NT does not stray far from the conclusions of Qumran and, in some scholars' minds, it even builds off these developments.[23] Whether or not a direct relationship between NT writings and Qumran literature is traceable, there are at least some common features that suggest a broader familiarity, and perhaps even agreement, with those shared concepts. Numerous sections of the NT depict Jesus as a Davidic figure who significantly reforms the temple system. In the Gospels, Jesus' ministry is decisively a *building* operation that coalesces in a new temple, the church. The examination of Matt 21 above has already demonstrated the continuity between the christological developments of the NT and the king-temple union of the stone testimonia. Likewise, John's Gospel emphasizes the Christ-as-temple motif by utilizing OT language to describe the nature of his arrival and ministry. Jesus is referred to as the *word of God* that *became flesh and dwelt among us* in John 1:1–4, 14. The English word, *dwelt*, is translated from the Greek word *Skēnoō*, and expresses Jesus' arrival in language

---

20. The interpretation of *rock of Zion* takes on a different meaning depending on which English translation one uses. While Vermes' translation seems to identify the rock as Jerusalem, Martinez's work points to the rock as David. Wise's translation makes the rock of Zion much more ambiguous where either interpretation is possible.

21. Translation from Wise et al., *Dead Sea Scrolls*, 256.

22. Wise et al., *Dead Sea Scrolls*, 257.

23. See Regev, "Community as Temple," 604–31.

similar to God's *tenting* among the Israelites in the OT.[24] The passage could be rendered, "the word became flesh and *tabernacled* among us."[25] John's placement of the temple cleansing early on in his Gospel demonstrates the theological arrangement he seeks to create. After referring to Jesus as the tabernacle in John 1:14, the Gospel goes on to connect Jesus to the sacred space of Bethel in John 1:51. Here, Jesus makes the claim that the intersection of heaven and earth is found in his body, where the angels of God can be seen "ascending and descending on the Son of Man." From there, Christ cleanses the temple in chapter two, following it up with the statement, "Destroy this temple, and in three days I will raise it up" (John 2:19). There is no ambiguity regarding this statement as John 2:21 clarifies, "But he was speaking about the temple of his body." It is also possible that the reference to *living water* in John 7:38 was made in Jerusalem, and the temple backdrop would have served as a mental stimulator for recalling the eschatological image of Ezek 47, where life-giving water flows out of the temple. Following this statement, the crowds break into an argument regarding Jesus' Davidic origin, a point to which they associate with his statement, and his identity as the Christ.[26]

Beyond the witness of the Gospels, a continuation of the messianic temple builder resumes in the NT. Paul and Barnabas, in Acts 15, defend the reception of the gentiles into the faith community on the basis of Amos 9:11–12. There, the prophet foresees a day when the "tent of David" will be rebuilt for the inclusion of foreigners in God's company. Paul goes on to write in his first epistle to the Corinthians, "You are God's field, God's building" just before describing Christ as the "foundation" upon which the church—"God's temple"—is built (1 Cor 3:9–16). Though he makes no reference here to the lineage of David specifically, his employment of the word "Christ" speaks implicitly of his Davidic lineage. Paul further makes these ties in Eph 2:14–22 where he reveals the inclusion of gentile aliens into the household of God on the basis of the Christ's work. Temple imagery is employed here revealing that the *implicit* Davidic figure is the *explicit* cornerstone upon which God's house is built.

The Petrine writings also perpetuate the idea that David's heir would restore the temple. Peter, like Paul, does not use language explicitly linking

---

24. BDAG, 929.

25. Gangel, *John*, 13.

26. For a thorough treatment of John's connection of Jesus to the temple, see Kerr, *Temple of Jesus' Body*.

Jesus to David—e.g., son of David, branch of Jesse, etc.—but he does employ the word "Christ" and quotes OT passages associated with the house of David. In 1 Pet 2:1–10, two cornerstone passages from the OT are quoted, one of which is Ps 118:22, a passage previously connected to the David tradition earlier in this chapter. The other cornerstone passage is that of Isa 28:16, which, if associated with the Davidic monarchy at all, is ambiguous at best. The argument made in earlier chapters is that the cornerstone reference in Isa 28 is to God's presence in the temple. If that is an accurate conclusion, then Peter is likely drawing from two cornerstone sources, one of which connects Jesus to David and the other to the temple.

Peter employs the cornerstone references in a temple-building metaphor that runs akin to that of Paul's in Eph 2. Jesus, as the cornerstone, becomes the foundational element upon which the house of God is built. Those joining themselves to that temple foundation inherit an assortment of identity labels that are laid out in 1 Pet 2:9, among which is the identity of a "royal priesthood." These labels are not insignificant, as they reveal qualities of the Christ that are being shared in this spiritual union. Peter states, "As you come to him, a living stone . . . you yourselves like living stones are being built up." Logically, if believers are identified as royal priests, it is an indication that this identity is rooted in the person of Christ who is both the Davidic heir and restorer of the eschatological temple. Therefore, Peter's use of the cornerstone intentionally draws upon the stone testimonia's associations to both the Davidic monarchy and the temple.

CONCLUSION

The identity of the rock has taken many forms throughout the history of Israel's sacred literature. And while there remains a common association with God's presence among each manifestation, the process in which the king assumes the identity of "rock" is highly significant for the progression of messianic theology. Regarding the evolution of these theological conclusions, NT scholar Gregory Lanier states, "Who is the stone? It begins in the OT as Yahweh himself, but it later develops through the canonical prophetic writings, the targums, the LXX, and Qumran literature into a messianic or kingly figure."[27] Ultimately, God is the king of the world (Ps 93:1), yet, those operating as regents of his reign reflect his majesty as well as the other divine attributes captured in the symbolism of the rock metaphor.

27. Lanier, "Rejected Stone," 748.

The Rock: The King

The beauty of the identification of the king as the rock lies in the subtle ambiguity of the Bible's witness. Though the royal figure arises within a monarchy birthed in sin, the covenantal progression that flowers throughout the revelatory process permits the reader to interpret past references with a more precise understanding. Those texts that would have been overwhelmingly associated with the temple, Jerusalem, or some other object in the past, can now be understood within a messianic context, all of which comes as result of enhanced clarity, not an objective shift in reality. What makes this beautiful is that it testifies to God's ability to speak volumes while we, the recipients, only grasp bits and pieces of what is revealed. It is as if God implanted a symphony of theological truth within a passage, and we have come to it initially identifying the arrangement as a three-part ensemble. Yet, as the biblical story unfolds through progressive revelation, the reader is awakened to the other instruments at play.

To further use the analogy, it is not as if God has started with a soloist, worked up to a duet, and finally reached a symphonic finale in the concluding pages of the NT, but rather, the full symphony is available from the first act. God has not changed his word, but we, as those experiencing the full progression of Scripture, i.e., the completed Bible, have come to it changed, reoriented, and enabled to hear what was there from the start. God has not kept truth under lock and key in the heavens reserved for a later time, but has "hidden" them in plain sight awaiting the adjustment of human eyes and ears through the expansion of divine revelation.

6

The Rock: The Kingdom

THE PREVIOUS CHAPTER EVALUATED the rock metaphor in terms of Israel's king and his representation of divinity. This chapter takes up another aspect of the rock metaphor that is closely associated with the king—the *kingdom*. As the king of Israel's purpose was to reflect God through the authority of regency, it was the purpose of the nation, or kingdom, to extend this representation to its farthest extent. In doing this, the nation would mirror the righteousness of the king as he mirrored the righteousness of God. Just as Adam was commanded to be fruitful and fill the earth with image bearers of God, the nation of Israel was now executing a similar purpose in their pursuit of a "holy nation" as a "kingdom of priests" under the rulership of God's anointed one (Exod 19:6). However, this model never reached its full potential due to the reoccurring perversion within the mirroring sequence described above and in the previous chapters. Though God's holiness never dimmed in the slightest degree, the kings who were appointed to reflect that holiness certainly did, as did the nation. A cursory reading of 1-2 Kings and 1-2 Chronicles will reveal the great failure of the monarchial system.

Nevertheless, human failure did not unravel the biblical purposes recognized within the dominion mandate, nor the various recapitulations of Adamic rule in Israel's history. As God continued to speak to the chosen tribes of Jacob, he revealed that the idea of kingdom expansion was still his purpose for filling the world with his glory. Though Adam and his progeny had failed, a king was prophesied to come and establish a kingdom that would truly reflect the attributes of the divine rock. This kingdom becomes another referent within the Bible to which the rock metaphor speaks. This chapter will examine the book of Daniel to highlight these developments but will also look to other passages and events within the OT record for additional support.

THE ROCK IN DANIEL

The book of Daniel serves as the main source for evaluating *kingdom* as an aspect of the rock metaphor. In a dream of Nebuchadnezzar recorded in Dan 2, a statue composed of differing layers and materials is reduced to rubble when a divinely crafted rock collides with the image. Daniel indicates that the materials of the statue represent various kingdoms that will arise in the sequence of human history, yet the end of time will usher in a kingdom superior to all others that will endure into eternity. The features of this particular rock not only validate many of the ideas concerning the rock metaphor previously mentioned in earlier chapters, but also provide insight into the latter stages of biblical revelation. Below, the direct references to the rock will be evaluated in relationship to the already established features of the rock metaphor.

The Rock as Kingdom

Daniel 2:34–35 states, "While you were watching, a rock was cut out, but not by human hands. It struck the statue on its feet of iron and clay and smashed them. Then the iron, the clay, the bronze, the silver and the gold were all broken to pieces and became like chaff on a threshing floor in the summer. The wind swept them away without leaving a trace. But the rock that struck the statue became a huge mountain and filled the whole earth." Here, and in other passages of Dan 2, the identity of the rock is explicitly revealed as a kingdom. Not only is the rock of God compared to other kingdoms, but Daniel explicitly describes it as being the kingdom that "the God of heaven will set up" (Dan 2:44). Though the other nations are represented by iron, clay, bronze, silver, and gold—each a form of earthen materials within the broader category of rocks—they are destroyed by a particular rock that is distinct in that it is not made with human hands.

The phrase "no human hands" indicates that the kingdom represented by this rock is from God.[1] However, there exists a degree of ambiguity in

---

1. Longman, *Daniel–Malachi*, 67.

that statement if no other clarifying remarks accompany it. What is God's relationship to the kingdom? Does he just create it and send it? Does he rule over it? To begin, the context of the chapter seems to indicate that a degree of synonymity exists between a kingdom and its king, allowing for an interchangeability of terms. Exemplary of this is the way in which each material in the statue represents a kingdom, yet the gold section correlates to the *king* of Babylon instead of the *kingdom* of Babylon. Daniel explicitly tells Nebuchadnezzar, "You are that head of gold" (Dan 2:38). Nebuchadnezzar, therefore, represented the kingdom of Babylon in this image, and it is likely that a rock *not made with hands* follows a similar pattern. God is the rock not made with hands—a king—but represents a kingdom.

This close association should come as no surprise since the rock has already been connected to God and the security of his reign in the previous chapter. The kingdom described here is a sphere within which God is present and reigning completely. Though God reigns over all the earth now, this particular kingdom will usher in a time where every other authority is broken down and removed. Therefore, God's authority will be the *only* authority. The Bible clearly draws these connections, but they are also observable in extrabiblical writings as well. The deuterocanonical writing of 2 Enoch states, "And who am I to give an account of the incomprehensible being of the Lord, and of his face, so extremely strange and indescribable? And how many are his commands, and his multiple voice, and the Lord's *throne*, supremely great and *not made by hands*, and the choir stalls all around him, the cherubim and the seraphim armies, and their never-silent singing" (2 En. 22:2; italics mine). Here, the quality of God's throne is enhanced by the absence of *human hands*, thus implying that his reign is unadulterated by opposing human voices. The same author goes on to write, "I am self-eternal and *not made by hands* . . . go down onto the earth and tell your sons all that I have told you and everything that you have seen, from the lowest heavens *up to my throne* . . . there is *no one who opposes me or who is insubordinate to me*; for *all submit* themselves to *my sole* rule and work *my sole dominion*" (2 En 33:4–7; italics mine). The writer explicitly draws attention to the *sole* dominion of God as the highest form of rule.

The Rock as Temple

While Daniel's emphasis of "human hands" certainly has literary connections to God's reign, the phrase appears numerous times throughout the

Bible within the context of cultic worship purity.[2] In Deut 4:28, Moses predicts that the Israelites will be scattered in the new land and will "serve the gods of wood and stone, the work of human hands." The Psalms employ this language where they describe idols made of silver and gold as "the work of human hands" (Ps 115:4; 135:15). The NT also records this distinction between God and idol in Paul's Mars Hill sermon where he states, "The God who made the world and everything in it, being Lord of heaven and earth, does not live in temples *made by man*, nor is he *served by human hands*, as though he needed anything, since he himself gives to all mankind life and breath and everything" (Acts 17:24–25; italics mine).

The book Bel and the Dragon is a work that also makes this distinction. This apocryphal writing reflects the life and circumstances of Daniel and employs the language currently under review. After Cyrus, the Persian king, questions Daniel regarding his unwillingness to feed an offering to the foreign god Bel, the prophet replies, "I may not worship idols *made with hands*, but the living God, who hath created the heaven and the earth, and hath sovereignty over all flesh" (Bel 15:5; italics mine). Here, the writer distinguishes Daniel's God from foreign idols in that he is not *made with hands* and is sovereign over creation. Each of these statements set God's prescribed mode of worship apart from the cultic behaviors derived from human innovation.

The biblical testimony is unanimous regarding the repugnancy of idol worship over the worship of God. To be "made by human hands" is to be inferior to the infinite God of creation. Even in the history of Israel's cultic rituals lies an undercurrent of theological disassociation with human contribution to divine access. Solomon's words at the dedication of the temple diminished the ontological holiness of the site by revealing its limitations as a man-made sanctuary. He states, "But will God indeed dwell on the earth? Behold, heaven and the highest heaven cannot contain you; how much less this house that *I have built*!" (1 Kgs 8:27; italics mine) Even as the sanctuary was being erected, the human element was drastically reduced. A prohibition was established in 1 Kgs 6:7 against the use of iron instruments within the sanctuary during the temple's construction. This prohibition not only reduced human noise from the sacred space, but reimposed the standard of holiness presented to Moses during the giving of the Law; "If you make me

---

2. For a look at how this idea developed in the OT prophets, see Barton, "Work of Human Hands," 63–72.

an altar of stone, you shall not build it of hewn stones, for if you wield your tool on it you profane it" (Exod 20:25)[3]

Therefore, Daniel's imagery of a rock which excluded the contribution of "human hands" stands as a literary symbol of divine reign and access. Daniel 7:14 elaborates on this, describing this kingdom as an "everlasting" dominion within which his people will serve him.[4] And even though Dan 2 is primarily focused on the subject of kingdom, the connotations of temple access should not be ignored. In light of the references above, it is likely that the rock—especially in the form of a *mountain*—carried the theological load of the temple within the minds of the Jewish audience. The trial of Jesus in Mark 14 provides the best evidence of this connection. One of Jesus' accusers states, "We heard him say, 'I will destroy this temple that is *made with hands*, and in three days I will build another, *not made with hands*'" (Mark 14:58; italics mine). The high priest goes on to ask Jesus plainly, "Are you the Christ, the Son of the Blessed?" (Mark 14:61). By connecting the title *Christ* to the accusation made, the high priest reveals some common association between David's heir and temple restoration, regardless of the priest's personal beliefs on the subject. Jesus, then, gives a response that is clearly an allusion to Dan 7:13, "I am, and you will see the Son of Man seated at the right hand of Power, and coming with the clouds of heaven" (Mark 14:62).[5] By claiming to be the Son of Man riding on the clouds, Jesus depicts himself as the king and the point of divine access, since he *is* the temple not made with hands. By employing Jesus' own hermeneutic, the rock in Daniel can be appropriately interpreted as a symbol of both divine reign and access.

ROCK AS AN EXPANDING KINGDOM-TEMPLE IN DANIEL

Since God's rule and temple-presence are both deeply rooted within the rock metaphor and language Daniel uses to employ it, it is likely that the expanding mountain in Dan 2:34 should be understood as both a divine kingdom and a sanctuary. The concept of God's global reign and access are not isolated to the image of Dan 2, but find parallel accounts throughout

---

3. Longman and Garland, *Expositor's Bible Commentary*, 681.

4. In this context, the dominion is given to the Son of Man by the Ancient of Days and later bestowed upon the saints (Dan 7:18). So while humanity receives the kingdom, it has God as its source.

5. See France, *Gospel of Mark*, 611–13.

The Rock: The Kingdom

the biblical corpus. The portrait of God reigning over the earth in an era of perpetual peace and prosperity is echoed throughout the Psalms and prophetic writings (e.g., Isa 9:6–7; 11:1–10).[6] As one continues into the NT, the abundance of references to the "kingdom of God" are staggering and demonstrate the progression of this theological concept throughout the intertestamental period.[7] Additionally, God's continual presence through a restored temple is an expectation that has already been traced in the previous chapter, but is conceptually connected to the idea of God's reign. As one reaches the conclusion of the NT, the convergence of kingdom and sanctuary reach their final expression: "Then I saw a new heaven and a new earth, for the first heaven and the first earth had passed away, and the sea was no more. And I saw the *holy city*, new *Jerusalem*, coming down out of heaven from God, prepared as a bride adorned for her husband. And I heard a loud voice from *the throne* saying, 'Behold, the *dwelling place of God is with man*. He will *dwell with them*, and they will be his people, and God himself will be with them as their God'" (Rev 21:1–3; italics mine). Here, God speaks from his throne as king and assures the redeemed community that he will dwell in their presence, providing them the divine access that had formerly been limited to the temple sanctum.[8]

If Rev 21 describes a global sanctuary where God reigns over his people, then Dan 2:35 communicates the same idea in a less-developed context. Through the use of stone imagery, Daniel portrays a rock that grows until it is a mountain that fills the entire world. While Nebuchadnezzar, Cyrus, and subsequent leaders each had a dominion that was far-reaching, and by some definitions included the known world, God's kingdom is set to arrive in a manner that surpasses their dominion in every way. Spatially, Dan 2:36–38 speaks of Nebuchadnezzar's authority as a global rule. Likewise, Cyrus' reign—a ruler whose kingdom is presumably associated with one of the *lesser* materials—is described in 2 Chr 36:23 as containing "all the kingdoms of the earth." Furthermore, Alexander the Great, who is likely depicted by the iron-clay mixture, has more notoriety for his global conquest than any other name in human history.[9] Yet, when the kingdom of

---

6. For a look at how the Psalms look to a day of peace, see Vos, "Eschatology of the Psalter," 1–43.

7. For an exhaustive study of the NT usage of *kingdom*, see Ladd, *Gospel of the Kingdom*.

8. See Beale, "Eden, the Temple," 5–31.

9. For an in-depth look at the national identity of each material, see Storms, *Kingdom Come*, 93–134.

God has fully arrived there will be no living being who has not come under the subjugation of YHWH's rule, thus making it spatially superior to every dominion of man.

In addition to the kingdom's superiority of power and spatial occupancy, Daniel also illuminates the kingdom's supremacy of *duration*. While each of the previous kingdoms depicted in the dream reach a definite conclusion to their temporal existence, the kingdom of God comes in the form of an *eternal* reign. In Dan 2:44-45 the prophet states, "In the time of those kings, the God of heaven will set up a kingdom that will never be destroyed, nor will it be left to another people. It will crush all those kingdoms and bring them to an end, but it will itself endure forever." The permanency of God's kingdom distinguishes it from the finite rulers of this world. The NT community built upon these anticipations which can be seen throughout their writings. Luke 1:32-33 states, "He will be great and will be called the Son of the Most High. And the Lord God will give to him the throne of his father David, and he will reign over the house of Jacob forever, and of his kingdom there will be no end." Additionally, Rev 11:15 adds, "The kingdom of the world has become the kingdom of our Lord and of his Christ, and he shall reign forever and ever."

Before these texts existed as a part of the Christian canon, similar ideas were already being propagated in Jewish literature and oral tradition. For instance, the Qumran document 4Q246 describes the emergence of a kingdom of tribulation that is vanquished at the arrival of God's kingdom. It explains that the recipients of the divine kingdom are blessed in that "their kingdom will be an eternal kingdom . . . The great God will be their help, He Himself will fight for them, putting peoples into their power, overthrowing them all before them. God's rule will be an eternal rule and all the depths of [the earth are His]" (4Q246 II, 4-9).[10] The deuterocanonical writing of 2 Baruch follows a similar trajectory to that of Dan 2 where he describes four successive kingdoms who are dismantled at the arrival of the messianic kingdom (2 Bar 39-40). The author writes, "And his dominion will last forever until the world of corruption has ended and until the times which have been mentioned before have been fulfilled" (2 Bar. 40:3).[11] One final example of God's supreme and eternal reign exists in 4 Ezra 2:34-35, where it states, "Therefore I say to you, O nations that hear and understand,

---

10. Wise et al., *Dead Sea Scrolls*, 347.

11. All pseudepigraphal translations are based on the work of Charlesworth, *Old Testament Pseudepigrapha*.

The Rock: The Kingdom

'Await your shepherd; he will give you everlasting rest, because he who will come at the end of the age is close at hand. Be ready for the rewards of the kingdom, because the eternal light will shine upon you forevermore.'"

These examples, and countless others like them, demonstrate that Judaism embraced the idea that a kingdom of God would arrive at the end of time. His kingdom would be superior to every human institution in both, power, parameter, and duration. The eternal kingdom is not only a portrait of God's never-ending reign, but also of the eternal access humanity has to the kingdom. Though it is truly a kingdom "not made with hands," that does not mean that there won't be hands within it. One aspect of this kingdom's superiority is the multiethnic presence under God's universal rule.

ROCK AS KINGDOM IN OTHER PORTIONS OF SCRIPTURE

Daniel's image of the rock-turned-mountain is the most vivid picture of God's expanding kingdom in the OT; however, it is not the only portrait of this kingdom, nor is it the only reference in relation to the rock metaphor. Additionally, Daniel is not the only one to make reference to an expanding mountain. Isaiah 2 depicts the day of the Lord through the imagery of a growing mountain that exalts the presence of the Lord above all other forms of security. The prophet writes, "It shall come to pass in the latter days that the mountain of the house of the Lord shall be established as the highest of the mountains, and shall be lifted up above the hills; and all the nations shall flow to it" (Isa 2:2). While Mount Zion is not currently the tallest mountain in the world, or even in its region, Isaiah captures the exaltation of God and his temple by predicting a day where the growing rock of Zion will rise above the other summits of the earth.[12]

The remainder of Isa 2 demonstrates the results of this enlarged kingdom. Suddenly the nations of the world learn the ways of YHWH by going *up to the mountain of the Lord* (Isa 2:3). Judgement comes upon all nations resulting in global peace as people "walk in the light of the Lord" (Isa 2:4–5). This judgement, however, does not appear to be centrally located in Zion—like a courtroom scene—but is some way connected to the spreading "word of the LORD" that issues forth from God's presence on the holy mountain.[13] Those opposed to God are hiding as his presence expands to

---

12. Motyer sees this as an expression of YHWH triumphing over the other deities who are associated with various high places. Motyer, *Prophecy of Isaiah*, 54.

13. Motyer, *Prophecy of Isaiah*, 54.

the ends of the earth. Men are described as entering into rock caverns, clefts of rock, and hiding in the dust when God "rises to terrify the earth"—an expression used twice in this chapter (Isa 2:19, 21). Though these rock formations are universally accepted as a form of security to the contemporary reader of Isaiah's day, the superior rock is exalted "against all the lofty mountains, and against all the uplifted hills; against every high tower, and against every fortified wall" (Isa 2:14–15). Like the earthen features of Daniel's statue, the growing mountain will bring them all to ruin because it is a rock not made with hands. Isaiah expresses a similar idea at the conclusion of the chapter, writing, "Stop regarding man in whose nostrils is breath, for of what account is he?" (Isa 2:22).

Isaiah's account of the growing mountain communicates several ideas about God's end-time dominion. On one hand, the destruction of nations and judgment of the ungodly are partially clothed in monarchial expressions. Isaiah 2:10 states, "Enter into the rock and hide in the dust from before the terror of the Lord, and from the splendor of his majesty," which emphasizes the royal features of God's judgment. Yet, the passage also highlights the centrality of Mount Zion as the house of God in the context of his dominion. It becomes necessary, as has been the case repeatedly in this study, to see God's dominion in terms of both a monarchial kingdom and an ever-present sanctuary.

Psalm 102 is, perhaps, another subtle account of this expanding mountain. The psalter writes, "You will arise and have pity on Zion; it is the time to favor her; the appointed time has come. For your servants hold her stones dear and have pity on her dust. Nations will fear the name of the Lord, and all the kings of the earth will fear your glory. For the Lord builds up Zion; he appears in his glory." The phrase "build up" here is most likely a general term for restore, however the text goes on to describe the passing away of the foundations that God has laid. The psalmist states, "They will perish, but you will remain; they will all wear out like a garment. You will change them like a robe, and they will pass away" (Ps 102:26). How does one reconcile the waning earth with the increase of Zion? How can the final verse of this chapter say God's children "shall dwell secure" if the sphere on which they live will pass away? It would seem that the psalmist intends to convey that one kingdom is put aside when another kingdom arrives.[14] In Daniel, this is expressed in the imagery of the rock crushing the statue and expanding to

---

14. For an eschatological defense of this passage in the context of kingdom restoration, see Witt, "Hearing Psalm 102," 582–606.

The Rock: The Kingdom

fill the entire earth. In Ps 102, the image is slightly different, but conveys the same thing. The current world will be replaced, *like a garment*, by a new era wherein the holiness of God extends to every region of man.

THE EXPANDING ROCK METAPHOR IN JESUS' WORLD

The passages above provide additional layers to the stone testimonia of the OT, many of which find their way into the theological developments of NT writers and their contemporaries. Two features in this rock metaphor become very significant for these writers: first, the idea of expansion where a small object grows to encompass the entirety of creation, and second, the concept of replacement where one system gives way to a new one. As the writers of the intertestamental period, and afterward the NT, engaged with these aspects of kingdom theology, they began to incorporate eschatological descriptions of the future kingdom and its temple into their writings. Their literature envisioned a Utopian era that does not arrive in its splendor through internal reform, but rather, through external substitution.

The expansion of God's kingdom is often expressed in ways similar to that of Ps 102, where Zion is the referent encompassing the world. Document 11Q5 from the Dead Sea Scrolls states, "How sweet is the *waft of your praise, O Zion, over all the earth*! . . . Embrace the vision spoken of you, O Zion, the dreams of prophets sought for you! *Grow high, spread wide, O Zion*; praise the Most High, your redeemer—while my soul rejoices in your glory" (11Q5 XXII, 11–15; italics mine).[15] The author of this text clearly expects Zion be a spiritual light to the entire world, but also speaks in concrete terms of its growth. Likewise, a vision recorded in the apocalyptic work of 4 Ezra also reflects the global dominion that emerges from eschatological Zion. Here, like in Daniel, a vision depicts the power struggles of various kingdoms which ultimately are reduced to dust—or ash in 4 Ezra—under the Messiah's arrival. The author writes, "And when all the nations hear his voice, every man shall leave his own land and the warfare that they have against one another; and an innumerable multitude shall be gathered together, as you saw, desiring to come and conquer him. But he will stand on the top of Mount Zion. And Zion will come and be made manifest to all people, prepared and built, as you saw the mountain carved out without hands" (4 Ezra 13:33–36). This literary description clearly builds on Dan 2 as both works emphasize the mountain of God as the instrument

---

15. Translation from Wise et al., *Dead Sea Scrolls*, 576.

of destruction for the opposing kingdoms. Furthermore, both accounts explicitly describe the mountain as a rock made without *human hands*, and while 4 Ezra makes no direct statement regarding the expansion of the mountain, it is *prepared and built* in such a way that it becomes *manifest to all people*. The passage concludes by describing the long reach of God's redemption as he gathers his dispersed people from the farthest regions of earth (4 Ezra 13:44–45).

In addition to the idea of expansion, many Jewish writings also build upon Daniel's replacement eschatology.[16] Though it is clear that many first-century Jews expected Israel to reach a state of glory through political reform and military prowess, there were a number of dissenting voices who anticipated this transformation through divine interruption at the end of time. The Qumran community was one such sect that had isolated themselves, primarily in response to the theological errors propagated within Jewish society. In this sectarian arrangement, they upheld standards of purity that they believed to be missing in the culture—particularly in relation to the temple and priesthood—and awaited a day in which God would disrupt the current system with a new creation.[17] A document called the Temple Scroll states, "I shall sanctify My [te]mple with My glory, for I will cause My glory to dwell upon it until the Day of Creation, when I Myself will create My temple; I will establish it for Myself for everlasting in fulfillment of the covenant that I made with Jacob at Bethel" (11Q19 XXIX, 8–10).[18] This text is representative of the Qumran attitude toward the eschatological hope for Israel which presents itself as a new creation.

In document 1QS, known as the Rule of the Blessing, the author addresses the Prince of the Congregation stating, "May the Lord raise you up to everlasting heights, and as a fortified tower upon a high wall! . . . For God has established you as the scepter. The rulers . . . [and all the kings of the] nations shall serve you. He shall strengthen you with His holy Name" (1Q28b V, 23–29).[19] This document points to the anticipation of the Qumran community for a messianic ruler who will purge the world of its evil and usher in a new era of holiness. Not only is the OT idea of kingdom

---

16. By "replacement eschatology" I am not referring to supersessionism (the replacement of Israel by the church) but, rather, God's replacement of the current kingdoms with his eschatological kingdom.

17. These ideas are best seen in document 4QMMT, the Sectarian Manifesto.

18. Translation provided by Wise et al., *Dead Sea Scrolls*, 606.

19. Translation from Vermes, *Complete Dead Sea Scrolls*.

The Rock: The Kingdom

replacement recapitulated here, but a subtle glimpse of the expansion motif is observable as well. The prince is lifted to an eternal height, is set on high, and becomes the ruler of the nations, all of which portray an expanding dominion that is comprehensive at the conclusion.

Though many of the Qumran writings referenced above lie outside the protestant canon, their purpose is to demonstrate that the rock testimonia continued to be a central part of Jewish thought. These texts bridge the era of time between the OT's completion and the events of the NT record, providing a glimpse into the continuity and progression of messianic theology. When John the Baptist and Jesus arrived on the scene, they did not have to develop these ideas from the ground up, but rather, built upon concepts already existing within the social imaginary of their Jewish world. John's plea to "prepare the way of the Lord" is rooted in his belief that the "kingdom of heaven is at hand" (Matt 3:2–3). God's arrival to end Israel's warfare, to gather the flock, and to demonstrate his sovereignty over the nations is a part of the greater context of Isa 40 that John recapitulates in his eschatological message to Israel. His aim, therefore, is not to establish a new theological system but, rather, to demonstrate that the existing expectations of God's arrival were materializing.

Likewise, Jesus builds upon the preexisting pillars of Judaism's theological foundation. Most of his preaching that we have on record focuses on the concept of the kingdom of God and often accentuates the features described within this chapter. The expansive nature was expressed when Christ compared the kingdom to a mustard seed and leaven (Matt 13:31–33). In both parables, that which was small and unassuming at first experiences a process of growth and expansion.[20] Furthermore, Jesus also described the kingdom as one that was outside the current system of power, and that would arrive in the future to replace the kingdoms of this world. Matt 24 is one of the most explicit portraits of how these eschatological ideas will unfold, as the chapter describes Jesus' second coming of power and judgment. It is no coincidence that Matt 24:30–31 connects these events with Daniel's prophecy, where the son of man rides on the clouds to receive dominion over all the nations of the earth (Dan 7:13–14). God sends forth his kingdom from outside the earth, and in doing so replaces the powers of the world with Christ's global dominion.

The ideas of expansion and replacement are both embedded within the fabric of Jesus' and his contemporaries' understanding of God's kingdom.

---

20. Blomberg, *Matthew*, 219–20.

The expectation of a kingdom external to the current power structures arriving at the end of the age was not the ingenuity of the Christian sect, but was, rather, a deep-seated conviction of many within Judaism who recognized these ideas as features of the OT text. Likewise, was the idea that the kingdom would expand to encompass the entire world. Though these two ideas existed in the literature of the OT, the NT, and the writings of the intertestamental period, the details of their timing and relationship to one another were cryptic. The timing of God's kingdom is a feature of eschatology that even Jesus declared to be an unknowable aspect of the last age (Matt 24:36). However, the relationship between replacement and expansion begins to reveal itself as the NT unfolds.

CONCLUSION

The rock metaphor is used to describe numerous objects that represent God. The messianic figure that will arrive to usher in God's rule at the end of the age is the rock, but the kingdom he rules over is also depicted with this language. The king and the kingdom were tethered in such a way that an identity of one could describe the other. The way in which both Nebuchadnezzar and the nation over which he ruled share a common identity in the gold head, mirrors how Christ and his kingdom share an identity in the stone testimonia.

The portrait of the rock reveals to the OT audience that God's kingdom will come with power and destroy the kingdoms that currently exist. This image should instill comfort and joy within the hearts and minds of those aligning themselves with his will. The same security that has been previously symbolized by the rock metaphor provides a new degree of protection at the end of days. The old world will crumble beneath the power of this kingdom and God will replace the corrupted power structures with a reign of justice and righteousness.

Additionally, the rock grows and permeates the entirety of creation revealing the kingdom's expansion and universal reach. The details of this expansion are somewhat vague in Daniel's account, leading many to make assumptions as to *how* the kingdom could grow to a point that it replaces the other powers. Certain sects of Judaism believed that God would enable the nation of Israel to achieve this expansion through political and military victory; however, others believed an achievement like this was only possible through the inbreaking of God's kingdom—the day of visitation.

The Rock: The Kingdom

Though the OT is ambiguous regarding these details, the trail of literature reveals a Jewish anticipation of a geographically limitless kingdom.

The concepts of replacement and expansion are tied to kingdom in Daniel, but find other expressions throughout the Scripture and extrabiblical literature. Many of these writers describe the all-encompassing reach of God as an extension of the temple in God's new creation. The imagery flows naturally from the biblical pattern as both the monarchy and the priesthood have ties to the stone testimonia. The temple, its foundation, and its mountain have been incorporated into the rock metaphor as these objects represent God. And, yet, the king and his kingdom have also taken a share of the rock identity as, they too, mirror certain aspects of God. In the next chapter, the amalgamation of priest and king will be a central line of thought in the NT's portrait of Christ. Jesus' identity will be examined through the careful lens of the stone testimonia for an evaluation of what the NT authors intended to convey to their contemporary audience concerning the Messiah.

7

The Rock: Foundation of New Testament Christology

THE PREVIOUS CHAPTERS RECORD an attempt to trace the biblical use of the rock metaphor in the OT. The biblical record provides a conglomeration of images and descriptions that make up in its totality what has been referred to as the stone testimonia. This *testament from the rock* is a mosaic of various objects which are distinct but are interwoven around the common thread of the divine presence. Though the primary referent of the OT rock metaphor was God, the identity was also used among special people and places that closely mirrored God. The temple, Jerusalem, the Messiah, and the eschatological kingdom of God are examples of these theological reflections.

The exploration of these ties began with the temple and worked backward chronologically to the point of creation. We then looked at the concept of God as the rock and moved chronologically forward in the text to other uses of the rock metaphor. Though, the chronological path used to explore these connections was somewhat unorthodox, there was a method to the madness. The chapters moving backward were primarily focused on the rock metaphor's connection to the temple, whereas, those moving forward examined the rock's connection to kingdom. The desire was to create two threads of thought that, while separate, had a common source. Since God is the rock, both strands of imagery began with him in the creation account. These threads operate in two entirely distinct ways throughout the OT; however, a progression of separation is noticeable as the storyline moves from Eden to the institution of the Jewish monarchy.

The Rock: Foundation of New Testament Christology

In Eden, Adam operated in the capacity of both king and priest. He was to have dominion over creation, which reflected his vice regency and kingly authority. Additionally, Adam was to keep and cultivate the garden, duties which have linguistic ties in the Hebrew language to the role of the priesthood.[1] Eden was a primordial temple-kingdom in which Adam was commissioned to be a priest-king, one who ruled for God and mediated his holy presence. Here, the aspects of kingdom and temple are unified, but after the fall these roles become separated. The pinnacle of their separateness is seen in the story of Saul, who, being a king, performed the task of a priest and lost his kingdom as a consequence (1 Sam 13:8–14). By making sacrifices that were unlawful for him to make, God discontinues Saul's reign over Israel and transfers it to David.[2]

The distinctness of the priesthood from the political rulers within Israel continues to resurface throughout the Scripture; however, the gap begins to close under the Davidic covenant. David is not a priest, nor are his immediate successors, but his connection to the building of the temple initiates a trajectory towards the rejoining of these roles. By the time the prophets begin speaking of an eschatological king, they do so in ways that connect his reign to the temple system (see the diagram below). Ezekiel speaks of the prince who will have access and responsibilities within the new temple, Zechariah describes a priest on the throne with the king and makes reference to a *crown in the temple* (Zech 6:13–14). The psalter also contributes to this merger as it describes a figure who receives a "scepter," wears "holy garments," and who is a "priest forever" (Ps 110:2–4).

---

1. See, Beale, "Eden, the Temple," 5–31.

2. It should be noted that David made an altar for sacrifices in 2 Sam 24:25, and many theologians see the disobedience of Samuel's command as the sole reason for Saul's severe punishment, rather than him acting in a priestly capacity. See Longman, *1 Samuel–2 Kings*, 135–36. However, David's altar is built at the command of Gad, a prophet, and therefore, receives divine sanction. Unlike Saul who disobeyed God's prophetic command, David would be in violation if he *did not* build an altar and make the sacrifices. This should be seen as an anomaly rather than normative. Furthermore, passages describing these *irregular* offerings and sacrifices may include the presence of a priest even if not explicitly mentioned in the text. Solomon's sacrifice in 1 Kgs 3:15 does not describe priestly involvement, but the fact that he went *to Jerusalem* to make the sacrifice indicates that this was unlikely an independent process. Passages like Josh 22:29 indicate that Israel understood the severity of making unauthorized sacrifices. It is in this context that Saul can be seen as violating the normative protocol.

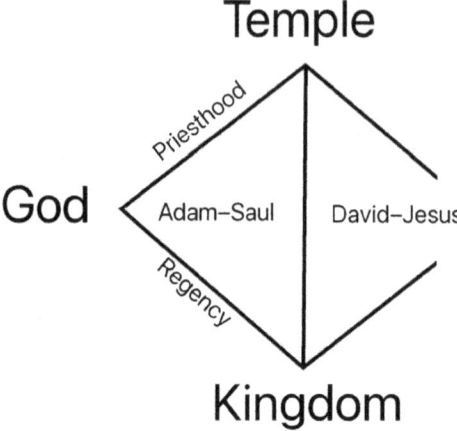

I point out these observations to highlight a general progression of thought that the reader of the OT should bear in mind as they enter into the NT text. This is not to suggest, however, that a clear portrait had emerged from this theological contour among the Jews of the Second Temple era and beyond. There are some who believed in two different messiahs; a king and a priest.³ Since both figures were anointed at the outset of their service, they both fit the description of *messiah* as the word literally means *anointed one*.⁴ Furthermore, God's promise of an enduring priesthood appear to be aimed at the house of Aaron while his king would have a Davidic lineage through the tribe of Judah. Even those in the Qumran community speak at times of plural messiahs.⁵

By the time the OT canon had closed, there was not a clear consensus within the Jewish community as to what the relationship of the king and the priesthood would be in the eschatological era. What can be certain is that the divide between king and priest began to thin. Some interpreted this era as a time of harmony between God's political ruler and his spiritual shepherd, yet, the NT writers come to a different conclusion. When Jesus accuses the Israelites of rejecting the cornerstone, he does so in response to their rejection of him as the Davidic heir and the true mediator of God's presence. The NT reveals that this rejection of Jesus was a rejection of king,

---

3. See Kittel and Friedrich, "χριω," in *Theological Dictionary*, 509–10.

4. See Ben Shahar, "'Anointed' and 'Messiah,'" 393–413.

5. 1QS IX, 10 states, "They shall govern themselves using the original precepts by which the men of the *Yahad* began to be instructed, doing so until there come the Prophet and the Messiahs of Aaron and Israel." Wise et al., *Dead Sea Scrolls*, 130–31.

kingdom, and temple. Any distinction between the kingly messiah and the priestly messiah that may have existed among certain segments of Judaism are ignored in the theology of the NT.

The office of king and priest existed as a unified part of the *imago dei* in the original creation. Though priest-kings operated within God's temple-kingdom at the beginning of time, sin created an environment in which the two roles were severed. Humanity's rulers, as well as their priests, were not only disjointed but sometimes outright hostile towards one another (1 Sam 22:17–18). However, the theme of restoration begins to visibly unfold under the Davidic covenant and the prophetic revelations concerning the Messiah. The NT writers make painstaking efforts to portray Jesus as the fulfillment of these revelations, describing him as David's heir and the restorative union of priest and king.

CHRISTOLOGICAL IMPLICATIONS OF THE ROCK METAPHOR

Chapter one provided an assortment of references that link Christ to the stone testimonia of the OT. However, the argument was made that those hearing these expressions today often lack the knowledge necessary to draw the proper conclusions intended by the original author. Our lack of familiarity with rock and stone, alone, is enough to disrupt the didactic function of the metaphor, but when coupled with a feeble understanding of OT Scripture and its theological contour, the hermeneutical challenges become staggering.

Since a metaphor only works when the audience has a working knowledge of the object and the symbol to which the comparison is made—God and the rock respectively—a lack of familiarity on either side hinders the transfer of meaning. Furthermore, the symbol of comparison may not be working solely on the basis of its physical features, but may also carry additional qualities into the metaphor given that there is a mutual understanding of these qualities between author and audience. In other words, God is not merely to be compared to a rock's composition, as we might understand it from a modern geological viewpoint, but must also be considered in relation to the mental, emotional, psychological, historical, political, and theological associations that were naturally present in the minds of the original audience as they reflected on these images. In the same way that donkeys and elephants have the potential for communicating beyond their biological traits in the American political mind, the rock metaphor surfaces throughout the Scriptures with an intense theological load.

It is my hope that the previous chapters have helped the modern reader recognize some of the theological baggage that may have been naturally embedded within the rock metaphor in the first century. This recognition will shed light on the NT's use of the metaphor and deepen their understanding of the christological claims that are being made when comparing Jesus to rock and stone. It is now that we apply the theological load to christological claims of the NT as they answer the question, "Who is Jesus?"

CHRIST AS KING

The NT account establishes Jesus as the Davidic heir, the king of God's people. Jesus is tied to the house of David in numerous ways, some explicit and some subtle, but the testimony of the NT emphatically portrays Christ as the anointed king.[6] Matthew 1 and Luke 3 provide genealogies that trace Jesus' family line back to David. Additionally, Jesus is called the Christ, the son of David (Mark 10:47), and the Lion of Judah (Rev 5:5), all of which assume ties to the covenantal throne. Furthermore, Jesus was born in Bethlehem, the city of David (Luke 2:11). A great portion of his ministry was focused on the exorcism of demons, which many viewed as a recapitulation of David's power over the evil spirit in Saul (1 Sam 16:23).[7] Davidic Psalms were quoted, and thus fulfilled, by Jesus, such as Ps 22:1: "My God, my God, why have you forsaken me?" The last chapter of the NT even states, "I, Jesus, have sent my angel to testify to you about these things for the churches. I am the root and the descendant of David, the bright morning star" (Rev 22:16).

Jesus' connection to the Davidic throne is explicitly clear in the NT record, but how does the rock metaphor advance these ideas? In chapter 5, it was proposed that the rock, as a theological symbol, had been utilized to depict the king. The rock motif progressed in the prophets and writers of the intertestamental period to incorporate the messianic reign of the eschaton. If this theological association was already present within the social imaginary of first century Israel, then any NT reference linking the rock to Jesus' kingship should be recognized and interpreted as an advancement of these already existing ideas.

---

6. Schreiner, *King in His Beauty*, 434–35.
7. See Duling, "Solomon, Exorcism, and the Son," 235–52.

The Rock: Foundation of New Testament Christology

Jesus' depiction of the two houses is a good starting point. The contrasted houses in this vivid portrait are illusory of one's obedience to Christ's words. Jesus states in Matt 7:24, "Everyone then who hears these words of mine *and does them* will be like a wise man who built his house on the rock" (italics mine). To build on the rock, then, is to listen and obey the voice of Christ. This form of obedience indicates that Jesus has come to rule and all who subject themselves to his authority are building upon the rock. Luke's account of the two houses further emphasizes this authority as he begins the passage with Jesus' statement, "Why do you call me 'Lord, Lord,' and not do what I tell you?" (Luke 6:46). The rock is the *lordship* of Jesus and is accessible only through submission to his rule.[8]

Matthew 16:16–18 provides another look at how the kingly association of the rock is employed within the NT portrait of Christ. Here, Jesus uses the rock metaphor to describe the church's foundation in response to Peter's confession. That confession, in Matt 16:16, states, "You are the Christ, the Son of the living God." While the modern reader would be quick to assume that this was a trinitarian confession, it is likely that Peter did not become *fully* aware of Jesus divinity for some time.[9] The concept of divine *sonship* was most often understood as an expression of *kingship*. David uses this nomenclature to describe his own reign in Ps 2:7 where he says, "I will tell of the decree: The Lord said to me, 'You are my Son; today I have begotten you.'" Second Samuel 7:14, Ps 72:1, and Isa 9:6–7 are other examples where sonship is linked to the reign of God's anointed king. While many of these references are evidence of Jesus' divinity within a postresurrection retrospective hermeneutic, it is most likely that kingship was the primary idea behind the phrase "Son of the living God" in its original setting.[10]

Peter connects sonship in this passage to the designation of Jesus as the *Christos* (Christ). This Greek equivalent to the aforementioned Hebrew *Messiah* points to Jesus' anointing as a declaration of his sonship and reign. It is likely that the Spirit's descent at Jesus' baptism served as the messianic anointing and it is here that God declares the sonship of Jesus: "And a voice came from heaven, 'You are my beloved Son; with you I am well pleased'" (Mark 1:11). God will speak audibly of his son only one other time in Mark's Gospel, where he states, "This is my beloved Son; listen to

---

8. Schreiner, *King in His Beauty*, 476.
9. Blomberg, *Matthew*, 250–51.
10. See Schreiner, *New Testament Theology*, 234–36.

him" (Mark 9:7) The two statements reveal that God views Jesus as the Son, or anointed King, who is to be listened to and obeyed.[11]

Even Jesus' enemies make this connection. Matthew 26:63 recalls the high priest interrogating Jesus with the words, "I adjure you by the living God, tell us if you are the Christ, the Son of God." Furthermore, those mocking Jesus at the crucifixion yell, "Let the Christ, the *King of Israel*, come down now from the cross that we may see and believe" (Mark 15:32; italics mine). These passages exemplify the common connection of sonship, kingship, and the Christ in the first-century mind. Peter's reference is unmistakably tied to Jesus' reign and it is upon that confession that the rock metaphor is employed.

Leaving the Gospels, Paul compares Jesus to the rock in numerous places and often refers to him as the *Christ* in these passages. Though the term *Christ* did eventually morph into a title rather than a description, the connection between Jesus as the rock and Jesus as the ruler is not solely based on this etymological tie.[12] Ephesians 2:20 is one example where Paul describes Christ's dominion through the language of the cornerstone. Jesus, according to Paul, has been seated at the right hand of God in heaven, "far above all rule and authority and power and dominion, and above every name that is named, not only in this age but also in the one to come" (Eph 1:21). Furthermore, God has put "all things under his feet" (Eph 1:22). This partial quotation of Ps 8:6 would have naturally carried the weight of the entire passage which begins, "You have given him dominion over the works of your hands." Paul intends for his audience to view Christ's work as a royal accomplishment, a kingly dominion.

This victorious reign is reflected in the cornerstone image of Eph 2:20. The cornerstone is the foundation upon which the church is expanded, a church that now incorporates both Jews and gentiles into its composition. Yet, Paul does not limit the imagery of the church to the cornerstone of the temple, but also describes this union of nations in the language of *citizenship*. Paul writes, "So then you are no longer strangers and aliens, but you are fellow citizens with the saints and members of the household of God" (Eph 2:19). For this group to be fellow *citizens* assumes that they

---

11. France, *Gospel of Mark*, 355. France sees the story as a recapitulation of Sinai and an "echo" of Deut 18:15, positioning Jesus as the *new Moses*. However, he also sees the language of sonship being an expansion of 2 Sam 7:14 and Ps 2:7, where kingship is expressed.

12. For a defense that Paul still understands Christ as a messianic identifier rather than a moniker, see Schreiner, *Paul, Apostle of God's Glory*, 76–77.

have obtained a political union distinct from the former tribalism that once created separation among those in the church. This political union can be none other than Christ's kingdom.[13]

Peter's description of Christ in 1 Pet 2:1–10 brings out this connection as well. Jesus is described as a *living stone*, the *cornerstone*, a *stone of stumbling*, and a *rock of offense*. The accumulation of so many OT references in one condensed location provides a glimpse at the unity of the stone testimonia and Peter draws off each layer to depict Christ's reign over his people. Those who stumble over the rock do so because they *disobey the word* (1 Pet 2:8). Those, however, that follow Christ and unite to him become "a chosen *race*, a *royal* priesthood, a holy *nation*, a *people* for his own possession" (1 Pet 2:9a; italics mine). They are a *race* and a *nation* because they find greater value in belonging to Jesus' kingdom than their earthly tribal heritage.[14] They are designated as *royal* because they belong to the king and reflect his majestic reign in their lives. The king now possess this group as his own because they are a part of his kingdom.

One more example of the NT's coupling of rock and reign can be seen in the book of Revelation. Though this final book of the NT is written in the cryptic style of the apocalyptic literary genre, there are certain allusions found within the book that are easily decipherable. In Rev 5:6, the author records a scene in which the Lamb of God is near the throne and is depicted as having seven horns, seven eyes, and seven spirits. The Revelator's audience would surely recognize the Lamb as Jesus Christ since this designation had already been established in earlier biblical writings (John 1:29, 36; 1 Cor 5:7; 1 Pet 1:19). Furthermore, Revelation goes on to describe the Lamb as having authority to open the seal and as one who had shed his blood to ransom the people of God (Rev 5:9). The authority to open the seals of the scroll is a continuation of Rev 5:5, which there depicts Jesus as "the Lion of the tribe of Judah, the Root of David." The Lamb and the Lion, therefore, are both references to Jesus Christ as each has the sole authority to open the sealed scroll. This authority is intended to highlight the kingly status of Jesus, a conclusion made obvious by the result: "And you have made them a kingdom and priests to our God, and they shall reign on the earth" (Rev 5:10).

As Rev 5 portrays Jesus as the king, it simultaneously connects him to the rock motif. The Lamb, here, is depicted as having seven eyes, which has no other referent in Scripture outside of Zech 3:9 and 4:10. In these

---

13. Leeman, *Political Church*, 323–25.
14. Grudem, *1 Peter*, 117–18.

texts, God provides Joshua, the high priest, with a stone that symbolizes the removal of iniquity. YHWH engraves the stone and it is described as having *seven eyes*. In Zech 4:10, an explanation is given regarding the seven eyes where it states, "These seven are the eyes of the Lord, which range through the whole earth." Zechariah provides a portrait of God's all seeing, all knowing, and all powerful character in the metaphor of a stone, and he does so as an encouragement to the Davidic king Zerubbabel who is restoring Israel. Through recapitulating the seven-eyed stone into the portrait of the Lamb, the Revelator presents Jesus as one who sees like God, enabling his people to "reign on the earth."[15]

As one makes their way through the NT stone imagery, the portrait of kingship continues to emerge within the literature. The OT backdrop provides a layer of historical context that supports the NT's portrait of Jesus as the eschatological king. By connecting Jesus to the language embedded within the stone testimonia, biblical authors sought to proclaim the arrival of the long awaited Messiah. They also sought to guide their audience toward a proper response to this recognition. One either received the words of Jesus—thereby submitting to his rule—for inclusion into the kingdom, or rejected the king like the cornerstone of Ps 118:22.

CHRIST AS TEMPLE

The passages above demonstrate that Jesus is the king, but running parallel to this idea is the NT's depiction of Jesus as the temple. Matthew, Paul, Peter, and John, each employ the rock metaphor in ways that draw upon the two threads of kingship and priesthood. Before exploring the temple associations of the NT, it is worth providing a few clarifying remarks concerning the matter. Jesus' connection to the temple is not metaphorically limited to one particular edifice—i.e., not just Solomon's temple—but incorporates the totality of divine access points into the comparison. Consequently, Jesus may be presented as the new temple, even if the tabernacle, Bethel, or some other point of divine access are used to make the theological comparison. While the NT authors often emphasize divine access in their christological developments, Christ's priestly work and sacrifice also serve as theological components to the Jesus-as-temple paradigm.

The writings of Paul provide several christological ties between the rock and the temple. One of the strongest connections lies in 1 Cor 3, where

15. Beale, *Book of Revelation*, 355.

The Rock: Foundation of New Testament Christology

Paul is establishing an ecclesiology of holiness for a congregation living amidst a pagan society.[16] In this context, the Corinthian church is identified as "God's building" and "God's temple," in that they have built upon the foundation of Christ. Concerning this foundation, Paul writes, "For no one can lay a foundation other than that which is laid, which is Jesus Christ. Now if anyone builds on the foundation with gold, silver, precious stones, wood, hay, straw—each one's work will become manifest, for the Day will disclose it, because it will be revealed by fire, and the fire will test what sort of work each one has done" (1 Cor 3:11–13). This passage speaks explicitly of Christ as the foundation of the temple and would have naturally identified Jesus as the cornerstone.

Additional rocks show up in this pericope as well, namely gold, silver, and precious stones. What is most interesting about this combination is that they are found together in only a few places in Scripture, one of which is the description of materials David had gathered for the building of the temple (1 Chr 29:2).[17] Paul's use of this combination of stones is likely employed to thicken the imagery as he describes the Corinthian church. The stones and structures that the early church would have associated with God's presence are now used in conjunction with Christ who exists as the foundation for the new temple community.

The second chapter of Ephesians echoes the imagery and Christology of 1 Cor 3, except here, Paul explicitly uses the word *cornerstone* to describe Jesus Christ. The general principle, however, is the same in both accounts. Like the parallel account in 1 Corinthians, Paul describes believers within a building metaphor, where Christ is the foundation of the building.[18] The building that is being erected is the temple, God's dwelling place (Eph 2:20–22). Paul goes on to use other metaphors throughout his writings but many of these run parallel to the ideas here. Sometimes Jesus is the head of the body instead of the foundation of the building, but in all cases, he is the thing that binds the church together into a unified whole.[19]

Not only does Paul utilize the stone testimonia to present Jesus as the cornerstone of the new temple, but he also establishes Christ's priestly

---

16. Fee, *First Epistle to the Corinthians*, 162.
17. Beale, *Temple and the Church's Mission*, 247–48.
18. Hoehner, *Ephesians*, 397.
19. Of the two Greek words the NT uses for *cornerstone*, Paul uses *akrogōniaios*, which can be rendered capstone or headstone. Akright suggests that Paul uses this choice as a double entendre to match the other metaphor employed in Ephesians—Christ as head of the body. See, Akright, "Role of 'In Christ,'" 147.

work within that context. In Ephesians, Jesus' blood is offered to reconcile humanity to God (Eph 2:13–16). And while Jesus' body is presented as the sacrificial component of atonement, Christ is also depicted as an active participant in the offering.[20] In Eph 5:26–27, Paul describes the priestly work of Christ by demonstrating that he *gave himself* to *sanctify* and *cleanse* the church by the *washing of water*, to present her *without spot or blemish*. While many commentators see these descriptions as references to the ancient "bridal bath" custom, there are numerous similarities to the Levitical sacrificial system as well.[21] The phrase "without blemish" is certainly reiterated throughout the book of Leviticus, as is the idea of being consecrated or sanctified. Furthermore, the ritual water cleansing is put alongside these elements in the instructions for dealing with leprosy in Lev 14. Here, the process for being made clean included *water washing* and the sacrifice of an animal *without blemish* by the priest (Lev 14:1–20). Another reason to identify this language with priestly antecedents is due to the earlier context of Eph 5:2, where Christ "gave himself up for us, a fragrant offering and sacrifice to God." Even if Paul's primary reference in Eph 5:26 is to the bridal bath custom, there certainly seems to be numerous passages in Ephesians linking Christ to both the priesthood and the sacrificial offerings. Paul could be employing both bridal bath and Levitical washing together—perhaps appealing to a water testimonia!

Peter makes similar connections to Christ, presenting him as (1) the foundation of the new temple, (2) a priest, and (3) the sacrifice. First Peter 2:1–10 portrays Jesus as the living stone upon which the other stones—a reference to believers—are built into a spiritual house. God's dwelling place, here, is a human building that is constructed on the foundation of this living stone. Peter does not leave these allusions to chance but provides direct quotations to connect Christ to the cornerstone of Isa 28:16, the stone of stumbling from Isa 8:14, and the capstone of Ps 118:22. Just as Paul recognizes that Jesus is the cornerstone and foundation of God's new building, Peter also advances this teaching with exceptional clarity.

In addition to these obvious connections to the temple, the greater context incorporates Jesus' priestly ministry. In the preceding chapter, Peter makes reference to the sacrificial imagery of the OT priesthood in his description of Christ's work. First Peter 1:18–19 states, "You were ransomed

---

20. Jesus is *making* (Eph 2:14), *creating* (Eph 2:15), *reconciling* (Eph 2:16), *preaching* (Eph 2:17), and *building* (Eph 2:20–22) within the body of believers.

21. Block et al., *Ephesians*, 178.

from the futile ways inherited from your forefathers, not with perishable things such as silver or gold, but with the precious blood of Christ, like that of a lamb without blemish or spot." The identification of Jesus as the lamb—as well as the phrase "without blemish"—draws upon the OT sacrificial system and prepares the reader for the temple imagery of chapter 2.

In summary, Peter makes a wide array of christological claims in a short amount of time. From the assortment of potential metaphorical associations that are loaded into the stone testimonia, Peter draws upon the entire gamut to present Jesus as king, temple, priest, and sacrifice. He also has much to say regarding the church, a topic that will be discussed in the next chapter. What can be said immediately is that Christ's place within the rock metaphor is the binding agent that holds the edifice together. The church is built upon Jesus as he removes their sin by his own blood sacrifice and makes them living reflections of his priestly and kingly work.

Revelation also brings the triad of temple, priest, and sacrifice, together into a harmonious christological portrait through the use of the rock metaphor. Where the kingship of Rev 5 was discussed above, the text also revealed Christ's priestly nature. The allusions to Zechariah's seven-eyed rock reveal the restoration of a kingdom, but also of the temple, as these two elements went hand in hand. Even though Zerubbabel, the Davidic king, was a primary character within the literary allusion, Joshua the High Priest is front and center within the narrative as well. Furthermore, the outcome of Jesus' redemptive work in Rev 5:10 brings the divided threads of kingdom and temple together in a victorious expression that mirrors Eden. Here, the people under Christ are a "kingdom and priests" to God, a statement that emphasizes the reunion of threads that were pulled asunder in the curse.

CHRIST AS TEMPLE-KINGDOM BUILDER

As the threads of kingship and temple begin to fuse, each element becomes indistinguishable from the other. While certain uses of the rock testimonia intentionally convey one particular aspect of its theological load, there are many instances where the rock metaphor combines a number of these elements together. This has already been demonstrated in part, but the fusion becomes even more robust as God's revelation concludes. Not only does the audience receive new images that incorporate the totality of the metaphor's significance, but these final revelations awaken the NT reader to a renewed understanding of earlier texts. That is to say, texts that seemed to only employ one aspect of the rock in its original setting may be interpreted differently in light of the finality of Scripture's testimony.

One example of this *expanded understanding* can be seen in Matt 16:16–19. Though Jesus' initial words to Peter may have been interpreted a certain way, the unfolding of Scripture reveals Jesus' statement to be loaded with theological implications that would have likely only been partially acknowledged at first. There is no way of knowing exactly what theological connections were initially drawn from the use of *rock* by Peter or the other disciples, but we can see that a postresurrection perspective of Christ and his redeeming work enhanced the disciples' ability to see the various implications embedded within Jesus' own words concerning himself.[22] The completed NT canon revealed, with even more intensity, the way in which these earlier expressions spoke comprehensively of Christ, despite the partial understanding by the first-hearers. In retrospect, those reading the Gospels with the advantage of the entire NT witness can see God's building plan in Pauline and Petrine sources and look for the development of those ideas in the more ambiguous statement of Matt 16. Likewise, the reader of Revelation, who finds an eschatological temple-kingdom conflated into one domain, can work backwards to Christ's earlier statements to see how these ideas materialized throughout the apostolic period. When this approach is pursued, Jesus' *building program* in Matt 16 becomes more than just an assembly of the church, but is the construction of a temple-kingdom.

In hindsight, we can observe Jesus' teaching on the kingdom and see how *his authority* is manifest in this building program. Jesus promises that the church built on the rock will withstand the gates of Hades and will also receive the *keys of the kingdom*. By wielding these keys, the church is able to "bind on earth" that which is "bound in heaven."[23] This same expression is used again in Matt 18:18 in the context of church discipline. Here, the church wields the responsibility of gatekeepers to ensure that the earthly manifestation of heavenly citizenship remains pure.[24] The authority expressed by these *keys* are tied to Jesus' Davidic throne. Revelation 3:7 describes Christ

---

22. John's Gospel thematically points to misunderstandings that are cleared up in the resurrection (e.g., John 2:22; 12:16). See Carson, *Gospel according to John*, 183.

23. The Greek construct of Matt 16:19 and its reiteration in Matt 18:18 employs the future perfect tense which is best understood as "shall have been bound" rather than "shall be bound." It is the church that is reflecting heaven, not the other way around. See Hagner, *Matthew 14–28*, 473–74.

24. For a thorough examination, see Leeman, *Political Church*, 294–316, 332–70.

as having the *key of David*, and with it, he *opens* and *shuts* with unchallenged authority. This depiction is borrowed from Isa 22:22 where the *key of David* is used as an expression of authority over David's house. Here, God's displeasure with Shebna has resulted in the kingdom authority being transferred over to Eliakim who now can *open and shut* at his discretion.[25] In summary, Jesus' church-building plan in Matt 16 resembles that of God's kingdom-building plan as seen in the Davidic covenant.

The ties above are a product of retrospect and cross–canon interpretation. Though it is possible that the statement in Matt 16:16–19 may have originally been received and interpreted as a description of God's kingdom, the illumination from these other sources remove any doubt. Furthermore, the way Paul, Peter, and John tether the idea of kingdom to temple should prompt the reading of Matthew to be conducted through a priestly lens. Matthew's use of rock is positioned in a literary bed of temple associations, both from the OT and the later NT writings, and should not ignore these associations despite the contextual ambiguity. Furthermore, the greater context of Matthew is an interweaving of kingdom and temple paradigms. Though Jesus preaches more about the kingdom than he does the temple, the *God with us* theme frames the entire book of Matthew and reveals that the kingdom comes in temple form providing humanity with divine access.

Jesus' designation as *Immanuel* in Matt 1:23 opens the literary account with a name that is conceptually tethered to the temple system. God instituted the priesthood and provided the blueprint for the tabernacle in that he might "dwell among them" (Exod 29:46). As the new tabernacle, Jesus is the dwelling place of the divine presence. This presence is emphasized again in Matt 18:18–20 where Christ promised, "There I am among you." The promise is given to the church and is contextually placed alongside their duty to act as gatekeepers for Christ's new community. In many ways this duty reflected the gatekeeping responsibility of the Levites who were tasked with preventing the unclean from entering the temple (2 Chr 23:19). The book of Matthew closes with the Great Commission where Jesus states, "I am with you always, to the end of the age" (Matt 28:20). Here, Matthew concludes his narrative by sending the church out to make disciples and promises to be with them as they carry out their duty.

The end of Matthew transpires in a way that very closely parallels the closing of the OT in its Hebraic arrangement.[26] In these final statements,

---

25. Verbrugge, "Power to Bind and Loose," 15–17.
26. See, Beale and Kim, *God Dwells among Us*, 96.

Cyrus, the Persian king, is releasing the Jews to return to their homeland in order that they might rebuild the temple. There it reads, "Thus says Cyrus king of Persia, 'The Lord, the God of heaven, has given me all the kingdoms of the earth, and he has charged me to build him a house at Jerusalem, which is in Judah. Whoever is among you of all his people, may the Lord his God be with him. Let him go up'" (2 Chr 36:23). There are three similarities between this account and Matthew's conclusion. First, both Jesus and Cyrus claim to have heavenly authority on earth. Second, both use language that compels the audience to go on the mission. Third, the divine presence is assumed to accompany those on the mission.

2 Chr 36:23	Matt 28:18–20
The Lord, the God of heaven, has given me all the kingdoms of the earth, and he has charged me to build him a house at Jerusalem.	All authority in heaven and on earth has been given to me.
Let him go up.	Go therefore and make disciples . . .
. . . may the Lord his God be with him	And behold, I am with you always, to the end of the age.

Consequently, it seems that the command of Cyrus to *build the temple* is being recapitulated in Jesus' words as he sends his community out to make disciples. The *God with us* theme at the conclusion of Matthew's Gospel is his climactic way of revealing that the expansion of the church is actually the building of the eschatological temple.[27]

In light of this hermeneutical thread, Jesus' statement, "on this rock I will build my church" seems to imply a building of kingdom and temple simultaneously. Jesus, after all, is the new temple and the Davidic king. These separate threads are seamlessly united in the person of Christ. Jesus is, then, the source of unifying power that was needed to reattach the various fibers that were ripped asunder in the curse of the fall. The creation that began as a temple-kingdom filled with priest-kings is being recreated in the new order of Christ.

---

27. See, Beale and Kim, *God Dwells among Us*, 96–97.

The Rock: Foundation of New Testament Christology

CHRIST AS GOD

Across the Scripture, the stone testimonia is developed through various referents that reflect God's holiness. However, the high Christology portrayed above seems to move beyond mere *reflection* to a more comprehensive form of divine imaging. While temples and mountains were *partial* reflections of divine attributes, Jesus arrives as the very imprint of God's nature (Heb 1:3). In Christ, all the aspects of the stone testimonia converge, even those strands that solely linked to the metaphor's depiction of God. The rock symbolized YHWH by portraying his creation, protection, preservation, provision, steadfastness, and salvation. As one examines the ministry of Christ, it is clear that Jesus fulfills each of these symbolic aspects. He is not only portrayed as the creator of all things (John 1:1–4, Col 1:16), but is also the inaugurator of the *new creation*.[28] The birth of the church is the manifestation of this new creation, and the resurrection of Christ served as proof that a new creation had begun.[29] His resurrection was the rebuilding of the new temple of his body, a temple that continues to be built in the expanding church. And since the new temple was a feature of the new kingdom, Jesus' glorified state should be understood as the firstfruits of all things new.[30]

Jesus also fulfills the role of divine protector, preserver, and provider. Previously, we examined how the rock of Isaiah served as protection from the storms of Assyria and other external threats. Though we made connections to the temple in chapter 2, it was ultimately God's presence that made this rock secure. Yet, in the NT record, it is neither the temple nor Jerusalem that are in view as the refuge, but Jesus Christ. It is Jesus' presence that accompanies the church on their mission. It is Jesus' promise that preserves the church in the face of death and Hades. It is Jesus' words that become the rock upon which the community can build their house. Repeatedly, Jesus is portrayed as the rock of protection, preservation, and steadfastness for the church.

The most prominent aspect of the rock metaphor in relation to Christ is his ability to save. His protection from the threats above are evidence that he offers the same deliverance described in the OT's use of the rock metaphor. Jesus is the cornerstone who provides the faith community with

---

28. Wellum and Feinberg, *God the Son Incarnate*, 116, 228.
29. See Emerson, *Christ and the New Creation*, 38–64.
30. Wellum and Feinberg, *God the Son Incarnate*, 228.

eternal security. He is the foundation stone upon which believers can build against the storms of Sheol. Christ is the cornerstone that plugs the chaos of death and darkness. He is the rock that followed the Israelites around in the wilderness and provided them with the water of life. He is the rock of Dan 2 that fills the earth with God's glory in the expansion of the eschatological temple-kingdom. He is the rock of Isa 8 and Ps 118, that crushes the sinful world in judgment. And though God's judgment would crush even the believer due to their sin, Christ is the cleft of the rock within which the believer finds shelter from the unbearable weightiness of God's unfathomable glory. Jesus is the seven-eyed rock that knows all, sees all, and sustains all. He is every rock in the stone testimonia, because every rock is a reflection of the divine presence, and Jesus is the very image of God (Col 1:15).

CONCLUSION

Jesus brings resolution to the biblical storyline by uniting the various strands of the rock testimonia. He recreates the harmony of purpose that was visible in Eden prior to the fall, but does so in a way that is telling of his true identity. By comprehensively fulfilling the symbolism that was associated with God—and the objects mirroring him—Jesus brings a symmetrical finale to the biblical storyline that attests to his divine identity. God began the story in perfection and holiness; it is only suiting that God restores it by way of a new beginning. Jesus, then, is not some external creature that comes to restore what God lost, but is, rather, God in the flesh reclaiming that which was his own.

The symmetrical comparison emerging in the use of the rock metaphor reveals that God authored creation while Jesus authors the new creation. God is designated as the rock while Jesus is designated as the cornerstone. God-the-rock saves from Sheol while Christ-the-rock saves from death and Hades. God provided water from a rock, but that rock was Christ who provides water for the believer's soul. These descriptions do not depict two distinct beings doing two distinct things, but illuminates the progressive cyclical activity of God in human history. Though it was hidden from human understanding early on, the triune God began the story, recapitulated the story in the form of history, repackaged the articulation of the story in literary artistry—i.e., the written word and the rock metaphor—and it is the triune God that finishes the story in the person of Christ. Nothing has deviated from the divine plan that was established before the foundation of the world (John 17:24, Eph 1:4, 1 Pet 1:20). God began something that he alone is capable of completing.

Jesus' identity as temple, king, and God are already well attested within church history and confirmed in modern scholarship. The rock metaphor does not bear any *new* information. However, these aspects of Christ's identity are often derived from systematic comparison of NT, and OT, texts. Though there is validity in drawing conclusions from systematic theology, it is refreshing to see that these conclusions emerge organically in the progression of the biblical storyline. In the next chapter, a biblical theological treatment of the faith community will be examined in the context of their relationship to the rock Jesus Christ.

8

The Rock: Foundation of New Testament Ecclesiology

IN THE LAST CHAPTER, we explored how the NT writers borrowed from the OT to demonstrate that Jesus was the messianic king, the new temple, and even the very God of creation. They often used the images and symbols from the stone testimonia to establish these claims. While these christological developments emerge in the recapitulation of the rock metaphor, the church is often portrayed alongside Jesus in these biblical accounts. If Jesus is the rock, what does that mean for the faith community? In what way do believers share in the rock identity and what are the implications for the church? Below, we will examine the various passages that speak to these questions and explore how the rock metaphor shapes NT ecclesiology.

THE CHURCH ON THE ROCK IN MATTHEW

The Gospel of Matthew has served as a featured portion of literature for exploring the rock metaphor in the NT. It will be used once more to develop an ecclesiological portrait from its use of rock symbolism. The three primary passages from this Gospel have been the teaching on the two houses from Matt 7:24–27, Peter's confession in Matt 16:16–19, and the cornerstone quotation in Matt 21:42. Since these contexts have been evaluated in previous chapters, I will not rearticulate those connections here, as important as that may be, but will assume the reader's familiarity with those earlier developments. Of most importance for the development to come is that the reader recognize the continuity that exists between these various rock references.[1] These three texts should not be viewed as a random assortment of disconnected speeches, but instead, an intentional arrangement of stories and teachings that advance the theological purposes of the writer.

A primary purpose of Matthew is to demonstrate that Jesus is the Davidic king and that his arrival marks the inauguration of the kingdom of God.[2] Statements like "but if it is by the Spirit of God that I cast out demons, then the kingdom of God has come upon you" (Matt 12:28) are indicative of this theological purpose. As the narrative unfolds, these ideas become more brazen in their development. At the beginning of Matthew, Jesus is a baby king who is helplessly dependent upon others to avoid being destroyed by the reigning tyrant of Israel. But by the end of the book, Matthew's development of the kingdom reaches its pinnacle where Jesus rebukes the kingdom and its practices. He denounces the political and spiritual leaders, including the temple system which had become corrupt (Matt 21:12–46), and then goes on to proclaim the outright destruction of Jerusalem (Matt 24:2). Jesus even announces that all authority on heaven and earth has been given to him (Matt 28:18), a statement that legitimizes and fuels the Great Commission as part of the kingdom replacement motif.

The advancements above are carried along in Matthew by his use of the rock metaphor. The progression of Matthew's ecclesiology begins subtlety in Matt 7:24–27, but becomes more pronounced in the later references to the rock. As one moves from Matt 7 to Matt 16, and finally Matt 21, the view of the ecclesiological imagery becomes exponentially clearer. While the *two houses* speech certainly reveals that it is essential to build upon the teaching of Jesus, it is not until Matt 16 that the reader comes to understand that the building takes shape in the form of a community. And while the threat within this passage *could* have had death in view—especially in light of the OT allusions underlying the passage—Matt 16:18 makes this assumption explicitly clear. By comparing these two accounts, we see that the truths in the former are present in the latter, except with more detail and precision concerning the church.

Matthew 16:16–19 is the first of three occurrences where the word *ekklesia* (church) is used in the book of Matthew, and is the only Gospel to utilize the term. While the *ekklesia* becomes a common identity label for the faith community in other NT literature, the early use during Jesus' ministry

---

1. Beale and Kim, *God Dwells among Us*, 88–89.
2. France, *Gospel of Matthew*, 25–26, 32–33.

Rock Doctrine

was likely ambiguous to some degree. When Jesus told his disciples that he would build his church, they probably heard this simply as development of a new *community*.[3] Ordinances, church discipline, and many other ecclesiological features had not been established, but were forthcoming even within Matthew's record.[4] Still, the parallel accounts of Matt 7 and 16 move from individual to corporate thereby opening the metaphor to the expanding rock motif as the community grows.

Peter is at the center of the conversation in Matt 16:16–19, and even undergoes a name change to reflect the significance of his own words. After confessing that Jesus is "the Christ the son of the living God," Jesus states, "And I tell you, you are Peter, and on this rock I will build my church, and the gates of hell shall not prevail against it" (Matt 16:18). The name Peter is the Greek word *Petros*, while the Greek word for rock in this passage is *petra*. Some have gone to great lengths to show discontinuity between these two words, often in opposition to the Catholic proposition that Peter was the first pope. However, the context seems to indicate that Peter is the referent in this context as the differences of the Greek words boil down to the gender values employed. While the word rock, or *petra*, is categorized as a feminine word in the Greek, and thus ends with the *a*, the use of *Rock* as a male name requires a masculine ending, such as the *os* at the end of *Petros*. All of which becomes even less significant when one recognizes that Jesus likely spoke in Aramaic and would have used the word *Kepha* for both the name and the word *rock* (i.e., "you are *Kepha*, and upon this *kepha* I will build my church").[5]

The protestant fear of associating Peter with the rock is misguided since this fact alone provides no basis for papal authority. Though the issue is outside the scope of this book, it is worth noting that the kingdom keys that are given to Peter in Matt 16:18–19 signify the heavenly authority that Peter personally wields in the administration of the church. When Jesus says, "I will give *you* the keys of the kingdom" and "whatever *you* bind on earth," he uses the singular *you* to refer to Peter in isolation from the others. Yet, two chapters later, this "binding" and "loosing" is expressed with the plural *you*, indicating that the entire church has been designated with this authority. The fact that Peter is called a rock does not place him in a

---

3. Blomberg, *Matthew*, 252–53.

4. Matthew 18:15–20 records the process of discipline and the Lord's Supper is instituted in Matt 26:26–29.

5. Schreiner, "Peter, the Rock," 105–6.

The Rock: Foundation of New Testament Ecclesiology

position superior to, or equal to, Christ the cornerstone.[6] What then does this identification of Peter tell us in the scope of Matthew's ecclesiology?

First, Matthew is revealing Jesus' fulfillment of the temple-building paradigm. As the new temple of God, Jesus is the cornerstone of that temple and the very presence of God. However, the building itself is not a building of actual stones but of people who are *identified* as stones. They are identified as stones because Jesus himself is identified as a stone. This resembles the mirroring of people and places in the OT that reflected God and assumed a share in the stone identity. Since Christians seek to *hear* and *do* all that Christ has commanded, they reflect his order and authority, and thereby bear his image. Many of the attributes of Christ become communicable to the new community on this basis. Therefore, Peter's accurate assessment of Jesus in his confession resulted in a natural *mirroring* of who Christ is. By reflecting the true nature of the cornerstone, Peter takes a share in the rock imagery. Peter's description in 1 Pet 2:4–5 reveals Jesus as the living stone, and the church as living stones. This relationship between the church and Christ will emerge repeatedly throughout the rock imagery of the NT.

Second, Matthew is revealing the expanding nature of the kingdom. Peter is indeed endowed with an earthly authority in this passage. He is even established as the rock. However, this rock is simply one among many, but serves as a foundation of the church in that it is a rock set *early on* in the construction project. In the same way a brick at the bottom of a wall is foundational to all the bricks stacked upon it, so is Peter to the church and the kingdom. This truth is set forth in Eph 2:20 where the building analogy places Christ as the cornerstone, but also states that the structure is "built on the foundation of the apostles and prophets." The apostles are also mentioned as having their names upon the twelve foundations in the new Jerusalem (Rev 21:14). These men do not replace Christ as the cornerstone, nor are they equal to him, but the apostles and prophets were the pioneers of the church. As Peter, and the other apostles, blazed the trail of evangelism and missions in the first century, they began a process that we continue today and are, thus, foundational stones in the building metaphor.

There are at least two places where expansion is noticeable in the Matt 16 pericope. The most obvious reference is Jesus' words "I will build my church," which assumes an increase through the building process. Another place that hints at the expansion of the kingdom is in the delegation of the

---

6. Context will not even allow it, as Jesus calls Peter *Satan* in this same chapter (Matt 16:23).

Rock Doctrine

kingdom keys. Peter and the early church are given authority that brings heavenly decisions to earthly expression. Jesus had already taught the disciples to pray "your kingdom come, your will be done, on earth as it is in heaven" (Matt 6:10), but now equips them to set the request in motion. Through the wielding of the kingdom keys—a symbol of authority that is likely synonymous with the authority articulated at the Great Commission—the church is sent out into the world to start building through evangelism and missions. Like the mustard seed and leaven parables of Matt 13:31–33, the rocky edifice of the church begins small but grows to incorporate people from every tribe, nation, and tongue.[7]

This movement in Matthew builds towards the Great Commission but uses the rock metaphor one last time in Matt 21:42. While this passage has been discussed previously, the emphasis in this chapter is the church and it is here that Matthew continues to emphasize the type of building that is being erected on the cornerstone. Through the greater context of the chapter, Jesus reveals that those building on the cornerstone are not a national-political entity but are, rather, a people from every tribe, nation, and tongue who receive the words of Christ. The Pharisees and other religious leaders who reject Jesus' claims understand that Christ is depicting them as the ones who stumble over the cornerstone. Matthew 21:43–45 states, "'Therefore I tell you, the kingdom of God will be taken away from you and given to a people producing its fruits. And the one who falls on this stone will be broken to pieces; and when it falls on anyone, it will crush him.' When the chief priests and the Pharisees heard his parables, they perceived that he was speaking about them."

From each rock metaphor to the next, the progression within Matthew develops a richer and richer ecclesiological portrait. The rock of Matt 7 revealed salvation through submission, while Matt 16 disclosed the corporate and expansive nature of the church. However, Matt 21 provides a clear depiction of the church as a multiethnic community that has replaced the geopolitical entity, Israel, as the recipients of God's favor.[8] Though Israel was

---

7. Blomberg, *Matthew*, 220–21.

8. The duration of this arrangement is outside the scope of this book. For those espousing a postmillennial eschatology, the conclusion would be that this is a permanent arrangement until the final state. However, those embracing a premillennial viewpoint would interpret this as a temporary disposition of the church age. Though postmillennialists will likely find the linguistic choice of "replaced" more palatable than the premillennial readership, I do not seek to use the word with the full range of eschatological baggage that so often accompanies the term.

set apart to be a kingdom of priests (Exod 19:6), the progressive nature of revelation suggests that this task has been shifted to the people of the new creation. Across the globe, the new temple grows in number as the gospel is preached and as new disciples are made. When one views Matthew's portrait from this vantage point, it is difficult not to see a fulfillment of Dan 2:31–45, where the small rock grows until it encompasses all nations.

THE CHURCH AND THE ROCK METAPHOR IN PAUL

If the rock metaphor is taking the shape of a growing human-temple that is built upon Christ, the Pauline literature plays a pivotal role in this development. Paul describes Christ as the cornerstone and a foundation, but these designations find their significance through the awareness of what, or who, is being supported. A king without a kingdom lacks royal luster and is, in many ways, no king at all. A foundation, likewise, that has nothing upon it is hardly praiseworthy. Jesus is no such foundation. Rather, the cornerstone image is repeatedly used in Paul to demonstrate the power of Christ to build up, secure, unite, and set apart those who trust in him. Paul uses the rock metaphor to identify this *building* as God's temple.

In 1 Cor 3:16–17, Paul explains to the church in Corinth that they are the temple of God. The same theology that was worked out with much labor in Matthew is now explicitly stated. However, the basis for their temple-identity is rooted not only in Christ as the foundation of the community, but also in the presence of the Holy Spirit. When Jesus made his statements in Matthew's account, the Holy Spirit had not yet been given and was, therefore, a minimal part of his description of the community. In Paul's account, however, the Spirit serves as an integral part of his ecclesiology and is cooperative in the building metaphor. Jesus is the foundation, but the Spirit works in such a way that the community is united to Christ and one another through his power.[9]

Paul aligns with Matthew where he uses the building metaphor to emphasize the church's corporate identity in Christ. Where he states, "Do you not know that you are God's temple and that God's Spirit dwells in you?" (1 Cor 3:16), the *you* is plural and indicates that all members of the congregation are a part of the building. Since the English language does not differentiate between singular and plural forms of the second-person

---

9. For more on the role of the Spirit in the temple imagery of Paul, see Hooker, "Sanctuary of his Body," 347–60.

pronoun, expressions like this have led many to believe that the temple identity is aimed at individual believers. While the Holy Spirit certainly dwells in individuals and even makes their bodies the house of God, Paul's use of the temple metaphor is employed to describe the communal nature of the local body.[10] These men and women are called to gather together, edify one another, and serve each other with a heavy emphasis on unity.[11] These instructions only make sense in a corporate setting.

Paul's use of the building metaphor in 1 Cor 3:16–17, 6:19, and 2 Cor 6:16 is primarily aimed at the church's purity.[12] However, Paul's purpose for describing the church as the temple in Eph 2:11–22 is to establish her multiethnic composition. He states that Christ has made Jew and gentile into *one body* by breaking down the "dividing wall of hostility" (Eph 2:14). This *wall* was likely a reference to the structure dividing the court of the gentiles from the inner sanctuary, but now, both ethnic groups find solidarity on the cornerstone.[13]

Paul's appeal to the Corinthian church for holy living is rooted in the fact that *they* are a temple in Corinth. In a world of Greco-Roman paganism, temples and shrines were spread throughout the major urban areas and Paul calls on the Corinthian church to be a separate and distinct temple that reflects the holiness of Christ.[14] This, of course, required an independent holiness as each member operated within the society, but the church was corporately tasked with the responsibility of upholding this standard of piety. Paul and Matthew both provide insight into how this was accomplished, and do so within the context of the building metaphor.

Parallel Content of Paul and Matthew

A brief look at how purity was prescribed to be upheld among the new temple community will reveal that Paul has not deviated from the earlier tradition, but has expanded the language and details within the Matthean account. For Matthew, the purity of Jesus' church was to be managed through *binding* and *loosing*. While the first occurrence of these terms in

---

10. Fee, *First Epistle to the Corinthians*, 159–60.

11. For a more thorough examination of the communal language employed by Paul, see Kirk, "When You Come Together," 34–60.

12. See Liu, *Temple Purity in 1–2 Corinthians*.

13. See Keener, "One New Temple in Christ," 75–92.

14. Fee, *First Epistle to the Corinthians*, 159–60.

The Rock: Foundation of New Testament Ecclesiology

Matt 16:16–19 is tied to the issuing of the kingdom keys with little detail or explanation, the second occurrence in Matt 18:15–20 is contextually rooted in a passage on church discipline. The removal of an unrepentant sinner from the community was one way that this authority could be applied. Yet, the passage is not solely about removing persons who fall into sin, but rather, restoring them to the community. It is no coincidence that the very next pericope is Jesus' lesson on forgiveness, and is a reminder that the keys are wielded for both binding *and* loosing—i.e., adding and subtracting from the community. Furthermore, these keys are to be wielded in such a way that they *reflect* the heavenly role of saints and cannot be seen as determinative of heavenly citizenship. While many translations have prompted such an interpretation—rendering Matt 16:19 and 18:18 as "whatever you bind on earth shall be bound in heaven"—the syntactical structure of Matthew's Greek here invites more theologically agreeable alternatives, such as the NASB95's "whatever you bind on earth shall have been bound in heaven."[15] This shifts the meaning from divine endorsement of all the church's decisions, to one of divine guidance, which better describes the relationship between Jesus and his new community.[16]

One thing that should be noted, is that a heavy emphasis is placed on the gathering of this community as they engage in the purifying process. In Matt 18, Jesus promises to be among the church as they gather to purify the body through discipline. The statement "for *where* two or three are *gathered* in my name, *there* am I *among* them" (Matt 18:20; italics mine) necessitates a physical gathering and promises a type of christological presence that cannot be reduced to the indwelling Spirit or the omnipresent nature of Christ's deity. Those types of presence are realities, even in the absence of a small gathering, since every believer has the privilege to walk with Christ. However, the promise here is towards the corporate gathering and must mean more.

All of this content develops from the dialogue of Matt 16:16–19 and is theologically downstream of the *rock* statement. Jesus is stacking stone upon stone in the building of the church, but commissions the participation of each stone in the process. They, under Jesus' direct, personal, and present supervision, follow his heavenly lead by adding stones that belong in the edifice, but removing those stones that do not reflect Christ in saving faith.

---

15. Gaebelein et al., *Matthew, Mark, Luke*, 370–74.
16. France, *Gospel of Matthew*, 626–27.

Paul also speaks to church authority in a similar way. In the middle of two prominent uses of the temple metaphor (1 Cor 3:16–17 and 6:19), Paul addresses the issue of discipline and compels the church to remove a member who lacks the fruit of a redeemed life. He states, "When you are assembled in the name of the Lord Jesus and my spirit is present, with the power of our Lord Jesus, you are to deliver this man to Satan for the destruction of the flesh, so that his spirit may be saved in the day of the Lord" (1 Cor 5:4–5). A comparison may be seen here between Paul and Matthew, that the corporate use of kingdom-power to remove those who do not belong in the faith community is transacted with the accompaniment of the divine presence. Jesus' statement "there I am among them" in Matt 18:20 runs parallel to the Corinthian church's assembling "with the power of our Lord Jesus" in 1 Cor 5:4. In both cases, the requirement of assembling emphasizes the local *gathered* church as the primary referent in the temple metaphor as it is this collective body that has the authority to build the temple—a service rendered even through the process of pruning.

Comparing these two passages accentuates how Paul and Matthew viewed the temple metaphor as an ecclesiological expression. In the same way the OT describes YHWH as dwelling among the congregation at the tent of *meeting* (Exod 27:21), the NT churches become recapitulations of that arrangement in their meetings. Christ is specifically *present* in the gathered assembly as God was uniquely manifested in the holy sanctuary of the tabernacle and temple. In this gathering, authority is extended to the community to *permit* and *prevent* human access to God's temple in the wielding of the kingdom keys—a responsibility reflective of the priestly duty in the OT. There, a member of Israel who was *cut off* from the community of faith would no longer enjoy the privilege of divine communion through temple access (e.g., Lev 17:10–14; Num 19:20).[17] Likewise, the NT temple—the church—had the authority to prune any in their ranks that did not exhibit a regenerate life, thereby restricting their *access* to this unique presence of Jesus. In summary, both Matthew and Paul are in agreement that the church community stands as a new iteration of God's temple, and progressively so. While the OT community had temple-access to God, the NT church *becomes* temple-access to God. Furthermore, the multiethnic composition of the new temple is an expansion of the edifice's inclusivity and accessibility.

---

17. In Hebrew, "cut off" can possibly mean "be put to death" but likely refers to exile since there are more direct ways of communicating the death sentence throughout Leviticus. See, Skylar, *Leviticus*, 258.

The Rock: Foundation of New Testament Ecclesiology

THE PETRINE ROCK AND UNION WITH CHRIST

Peter's use of the rock metaphor probably speaks to ecclesiology even more than it does Christology. Though Jesus is associated, in 1 Pet 2, with numerous passages from the OT stone testimonia, these expressions serve as the basis for *what* and *who* the church is. As one looks at the assortment of characteristics that describe the church in Peter's First Epistle, it becomes clear that the characteristics mirror that of Christ. We've previously discussed the idea of mirroring in the examination of the OT, where people, places, and objects find a share alongside God in the rock metaphor to the extent that they mirror him. A similar feature is noticeable here in the church's mirroring of Christ.

To set up the discussion, 1 Pet 2:1–12 describes a faith community that is depicted as (1) living stones; (2) a spiritual house; (3) a holy priesthood; (4) a chosen race; (5) a royal priesthood; (6) a holy nation; and (8) a people for his own possession. Among these designations, a clear reflection of the Messiah is observable since he, too, is depicted through many of these symbols and expressions. Throughout 1 Peter alone, Jesus is called *holy* (1 Pet 1:15–16, 3:15), described as a *living stone* (1 Pet 2:4), declared to be *chosen* by God (1 Pet 2:4, 6), portrayed as one associated with *priestly* sacrifices (1 Pet 1:19, 2:24), and designated the *cornerstone* of Zion (1 Pet 2:6–7), an expression with clear theological and contextual ties to the temple. How, then, do these designations become shared between Christ and his church? The answer begins with the concept of mirroring, but extends even further into the doctrine of *union with Christ*.

When 1 Pet 1:15 states, "But as he who called you is holy, you also be holy in all your conduct," the function of mirroring is certainly front and center. However, the ability to mirror the holiness of Christ and reflect his perfection lies outside the realm of human possibility. Humanity cannot become the dwelling place of God, a holy priesthood, or any number of the characteristics attributed to them in Scripture, through strength and desire alone, but experiences these features of the new creation through the union between believer and Savior.[18]

A full theological treatment of the union with Christ doctrine is beyond the scope of this book but deserves a cursory description to move forward with the ecclesiological assumptions wrought by the rock metaphor.

---

18. For more on union with Christ in 1 Peter, see Christensen, "Reborn Participants in Christ," 339–54.

Rock Doctrine

The Bible emphatically describes the believer as being united with Christ through various expressions. Christians are said to be "in Christ," to be "with Christ," to have Christ "in them," and to operate "through Christ," all of which portray a unity of distinct persons.[19] Jesus told his disciples, "Abide in me, and I in you. As the branch cannot bear fruit by itself, unless it abides in the vine, neither can you, unless you abide in me" (John 15:4). In these expressions, the idea emerges that individuals can connect themselves to Christ through faith and, consequently, receive certain qualities that were naturally not their own.

It is the doctrine of union with Christ that explains how believers are declared righteous, as the righteousness of Christ is imputed upon them. It is this same doctrine that explains believers' access to God, despite human sinfulness. Since Christ is seated at the right hand of God in heavenly places (Eph 1:20), Christians too are described as being seated with him in heavenly places. Though the church may be physically present on the earth, they are seated in the heavens "in Christ Jesus" (Eph 2:6). Jesus' access and proximity to God become an attribute of the believing community because of the oneness that exists between Christ and his church. There are certainly some qualities that are not shared in this union, such as Jesus' deity, but those that are reveal the unity of Jesus and his bride.

It is this concept that bleeds through in the evaluation of Peter's ecclesiology and his use of the rock metaphor. The church is described as living stones precisely because Jesus is a living stone. When Jesus identified Peter as the rock in Matt 16:18, Peter did not receive this title as a unique identity for himself, but communicates in this epistle that all within the believing community are rocks. They are built up, stone upon stone, into God's house because Jesus' body is the very dwelling place of God. The church, in 1 Pet 2:5, does not offer priestly sacrifices on her own authority, but rather, renders this service *because* Jesus is a high priest who offered himself as a sacrifice to God. Every biblical proposition that accentuates an aspect of the church's identity flows from her union with Christ.

Where the church is described as a *royal priesthood*, Peter is importing nomenclature from an OT setting upon the NT community. Israel was set apart to be a "kingdom of priests" (Exod 19:6), but this concept never fully materialized under the old covenant. While the Israelites had kings and priests, they never fulfilled the global commission for being a priest-king

---

19. For a thorough examination of these phrases and others similar to them, see Campbell, *Union with Christ*.

witness to the nations. Like Adam—who was supposed to fill the world with image bearers—Israel was supposed to mediate the presence of God to the world. She not only failed to do this, but did not even uphold the standard of purity and holiness within her own borders. It is not until Christ arrives that the vision for priestly and kingly faithfulness is fulfilled. Christ's authority and mediation were perfectly combined in his earthly ministry, and in fulfilling these human purposes, he accomplished what was intended for mankind from the beginning. Though Jesus did not leave the immediate area of Palestine, his global commission and spiritual indwelling provided the necessary "infrastructure" for the church to expand his accomplishment to all nations.

This background is reiterated here to illustrate that even designations like "royal priesthood" flow from the church's union with Christ. Furthermore, the christological roles of king and priest represent two primary threads of the stone testimonia that remained separate throughout the OT, but are now merged in Christ and his body. Ecclesiology, then, becomes a vital component to the symmetrical shape of human history. The union between God and his priest-kings in Eden has been restored, and thus mirrored, through Jesus and his church. The mission to fill the earth with image bearers is now underway and is a central component within Peter's theological instruction to a globally dispersed group of saints who make up his audience (1 Pet 1:1).[20]

ROCKS AND THE CHURCH IN REVELATION

The book of Revelation provides a variety of statements that directly—and some that indirectly—tie the faith community to the rock metaphor. Many of the rock references occur in a setting that continue to develop the themes of priesthood and kingdom. As cryptic as the book of Revelation may be at times, this thematic development within John's writing is not hidden. The first chapter begins with the statement, "To him who loves us and has freed us from our sins by his blood and made us a *kingdom, priests to his God* and Father, to him be glory and dominion forever and ever" (Rev 1:5; italics mine). The priest-king motif is revealed early to establish a hermeneutical pattern for reading the remainder of the book. A similar reference reoccurs in chapter 5 where John states, "You ransomed people for God from every tribe and language and people and nation, and you have made

---

20. Schreiner, *1, 2 Peter, Jude*, 41.

them a *kingdom and priests* to our God, and they shall reign on the earth" (Rev 5:9–10; italics mine). In the final chapters of the book, another explicit reference is provided: "Blessed and holy is the one who shares in the first resurrection! Over such the second death has no power, but they will be priests of God and of Christ, and they will reign with him for a thousand years" (Rev 20:6). With these passages in mind, the various rock references can naturally be interpreted within this paradigmatic context.[21]

John begins by portraying Jesus as a figure among seven golden lampstands, and these lampstands are identified as the seven churches. Since the lampstand served as a significant furnishing within the Holy Place, the ecclesiological connection to the temple is naturally present in the literary image (Exod 26:34–35). Revelation 3:12 advances this theme where the victors among the church at Philadelphia are designated as "a pillar in the temple" of God. It is even possible that the white stone given to the church of Pergamum in Rev 2:17 intentionally alludes to the stones of the priestly ephod.[22] In Exod 28:9–12, instruction was given to engrave two onyx stones with the names of the sons of Israel and they were to be attached to the ephod of the priest in order that he might "bear their names before the Lord." If this is the allusion intended, then the Pergamum church receives a priestly stone to bear before God in conjunction with their priestly duty.

The priest motif is intermingled with the reign of the church throughout the book. In the previous chapter we discussed the seven-eyed rock of Zechariah and the possible allusion to this text in Rev 5. The Lamb, here, has seven horns with seven eyes and seven spirits. The repeated use of *seven* emphasizes completeness and, based on Zech 4:10, describe Jesus' complete reign on the earth. However, the union with Christ theme that has become so prevalent at this point in the NT results in a shared reign among those who are united to him in saving faith. Because of the Lamb's sacrifice and subsequent reign, the saints are depicted as a ransomed kingdom with authority to "reign on the earth."

As the book unfolds, it is clear that the church has engaged in a priest–king mission that is successful. Revelation 7:9 describes a setting where representatives from every *tribe, nation,* and *tongue* surround the throne of God and worship the Lamb. The final stage of history also captures the success of the Great Commission where "the nations walk, and the kings of the earth will bring their glory into it" (Rev 21:24). Following

---

21. Beale, *Book of Revelation*, 193.
22. See, Osborne, *Revelation*, 240–42.

The Rock: Foundation of New Testament Ecclesiology

the pattern established in Daniel, Matthew, Paul, and Peter, the church is likewise portrayed by John as a growing structure that reaches globally in her mediatory role. Through much suffering and trial, the church arrives at the eternal state as a multiethnic kingdom and priesthood.

Throughout the NT, the church is presented as the temple of God and is therefore, the place where heaven and earth converge. I have argued extensively elsewhere that Jesus' unique temple-presence is manifest in the physical gathering of the saints, and is the most potent replication of the temple experience.[23] Therefore, as the church expands and spreads throughout the world, the temple grows in terms of physical presence. Consequently, there are more spaces where heaven meets earth today than ever existed during the biblical era, since church communities have spread to the ends of the earth. Yet, there are still places that do not provide this sort of access, either because of the lack of a Christian congregation, or simply a lack of people in general. The peak of Mount Everest, for instance, is not a place where heaven and earth converge, since no congregation gathers there in reflection of Christ's heavenly authority. However, Rev 21 reveals that a time is coming where the entire earth—every square inch of it—will become combined with heaven. There will no longer be a heaven and an earth, but only a heavenly earth.

The new Jerusalem in Rev 21 is a description of this era and reveals a world that exists in whole as the church did in part. Interestingly enough, the rock usage within this context continues to communicate the various strands of the rock testimonia that have been prevalent throughout this study. First, the new Jerusalem is depicted as a mountain, which should not be too shocking considering that the first Jerusalem was a mountain (Rev 21:10). However, the OT depictions of the restored kingdom and priesthood were highly developed alongside the concept of *Zion*. Furthermore, the reference to the mountain city as *great*, *high*, and *holy* have biblical connections to Zion from passages like Ps 48:1, Isa 40:9, and Ezek 40:2.[24]

Next, the foundation of the new Jerusalem is depicted as containing an assortment of precious jewels: "The foundations of the wall of the city were adorned with every kind of jewel. The first was jasper, the second sapphire, the third agate, the fourth emerald, the fifth onyx, the sixth carnelian, the seventh chrysolite, the eighth beryl, the ninth topaz, the tenth chrysoprase, the eleventh jacinth, the twelfth amethyst" (Rev 21:19–20). These precious

---

23. Crawford, *Where Has Sacred Space Gone?*
24. Beale, *Book of Revelation*, 1065.

rocks are not solely here to express the value of the new Jerusalem, but carry a heavy theological load. In Rev 4:2–3, John describes the heavenly throne of God which has the appearance of *jasper, carnelian,* and *emerald.* Here, John is borrowing from Ezekiel's vision of God which also depicts the divine presence through the use of precious stones (Ezek 1:26–28).[25] The use of precious stones, however, are not original in Ezekiel but have an earlier antecedent in the breastpiece of the priests, which had twelve precious stones set within (Exod 28:15–30).[26] Furthermore, these stones likely served as a reminder of Eden, where precious stones first existed within the temple-kingdom context of paradise (Gen 2:10–14; Ezek 28:13).

These connections, as were brought out in chapter 4, reveal the divine presence. Though the priests, and the new priesthood of the church, served in a mediatorial role to provide access to the divine presence in their respective contexts, the new Jerusalem is the place where God dwells with man. The stones in the ground demonstrate that the earth *is* heavenly access. There is no place on the new earth that escapes this temple-presence of God. This point is further solidified where John writes, "And I saw no temple in the city, for its temple is the Lord God the Almighty and the Lamb" (Rev 21:22). Since all of the new Jerusalem exists as a conflation of heaven and earth, there is no need for a temple because the entire world is the temple.

A third and final connection to the rock motif is directly tied to the absence of the temple. Among the various promises made to the churches in the opening chapters of Revelation lies a statement directly tied to the new Jerusalem. Revelation 3:12 states, "The one who conquers, I will make him a pillar in the temple of my God. Never shall he go out of it, and I will write on him the name of my God, and the name of the city of my God, the new Jerusalem, which comes down from my God out of heaven, and my own new name." Here, the conqueror is promised to be a pillar in the temple of God in the new Jerusalem, yet we've just seen that there is no temple in the new Jerusalem. To reconcile these two ideas, it is best to understand the absence of the temple as an expression regarding manmade structures. There is no need for a temple building to commune with God—i.e., to access heaven—since heaven and earth have merged into one geographical location, the entirety of the new heaven and earth. Therefore, those who exist as *pillars in the temple* are simply being designated as pillars

---

25. Beale, *Book of Revelation*, 320–21, and Schreiner, *New Testament Theology*, 164.
26. See Beale, *Temple and the Church's Mission*, 39–45.

within the new creation, not a physical edifice. Revelation 21:12–14 reveals that various features of the city are established with the inscription of human names. Gates and walls bear the names of the tribes of Israel and the twelve apostles of the Lamb.

It is likely, that the imagery invites the Christian reader to understand that they are among those whose names are written within the city. As members of Christ's church, they have participated in the expansion of the rock through kingdom suffering and the mediatorial process.[27] As others have come to faith through their priest-king work, they are built upon Jesus, the foundation. The same imagery used in Peter and Paul to depict the church as a temple is likely lying behind the social imaginary of the new covenant community as they read these descriptions. Though the absence of the physical temple is a definite feature of the New Jerusalem, God and the Lamb *are* the temple, and all who are united to the Lamb have a share in this identity.

Even following the judgment and the commencement of the eternal state, the church community continues their role of being priests and kings. Just as the duty was valid in a pre-fall Eden, it continues to exist into eternity despite the absence of sin and spiritual division between God and humanity. Revelation 22:3–5 states, "No longer will there be anything accursed, but the throne of God and of the Lamb will be in it, and his servants will worship him. They will see his face, and his name will be on their foreheads. And night will be no more. They will need no light of lamp or sun, for the Lord God will be their light, and they will reign forever and ever." This passage emphasizes the ongoing *reign* of the citizens—a point also observed in Rev 21:24—but simultaneously points to the *priestly* identity of the saints. The name of God on the forehead is an image that comes from Exod 28:36–38, where the name of YHWH is inscribed upon the head dress of the high priest.[28] Furthermore, the phrase "his servants will worship him" utilizes the Greek word *latreuō*, which emphasizes *service* more than generic *worship*.[29] This word often describes one's action before God and is frequently employed in the exchange between Moses and Pharaoh in the LXX. Moses' request for the Jews' freedom is rooted in the need to *serve* (*latreuoō*) God, and was based on the divine command "you shall *serve* God on this mountain" (Exod 3:12; italics mine). The word even emerges

---

27. For look at the church's suffering, see Marsh, "On Account of My Name," 671–84.
28. Beale, *Book of Revelation*, 295, 1112–14.
29. See Kirk, "When You Come Together," 45–46.

in a more technical sense in Num 16:9 where God highlights the Levitical role of *service* and *ministry* within the tabernacle.

In summary, the book of Revelation highlights the priest-king work of Christ, but also reveals the share believers have in this ministry as a result of their spiritual union. Jesus' reign on the earth, as well as the mediatorial role he assumed as the living temple of God, have become attributes theologically associated with the body of Christ. As believers commit themselves to the work of Christ, they become a part of a community that houses the very presence of God. The rock imagery employed by John reveals that believers are priests, kings, and foundational components in the new temple of God. The presence of God accompanies these saints in their earthly mission, and though the church suffers—as Christ did—the temple expands to include people from every tribe, tongue, and nation. In fulfillment of Dan 2, the finale of redemptive history is depicted as a glorious arrival of God's temple-kingdom, where believers constantly experience the presence of God, but continue to reign and serve with him. Daniel's expanding rock finally reaches its completion, as all creation is filled with the associations of the stone testimonia. Wherever the saints go, they will be in the presence of God, who will make his dwelling with men. Wherever the saints go, they will be in the presence of the king, who shines on them like the sun (Rev 21:23). Wherever the saints go, they will be within the precinct of the temple—since God and the Lamb are the temple (Rev 21:22). Wherever the saints go, they will be treading upon the new Jerusalem, the mountain of God, the eternal Zion.

CONCLUSION

The ecclesiology of the NT is significantly dependent upon the use of rock imagery. Matthew, Paul, Peter, and John each shape the identity and purpose of the church through their employment of the rock metaphor and establish the institution as a reflection of Christ. The doctrine of union with Christ emerges as an important concept for identifying not only what the church is, but how she obtained her various qualities. Though Jesus is the true rock—a feature of his divinity—the church assumes a part in the rock identity through her union to the Son of God. Members of the Christian community are depicted as carrying out the work of Christ, who was both priest and king. This priest-king function works towards a greater fulfillment of earlier iterations of the rock testimonia, specifically that of Daniel who records the expanding nature of the rock to reach global proportions.

Each believer, then, exists as a building block in the expanding edifice. Their priest-king service is delineated in the Great Commission and involves becoming a part of a structure that others can build on. By bearing those who come after them, the faith community participates in an ongoing effort that will permeate the various regions of the world. The glimpse of the eschatological community in Revelation reveals that the current efforts described in the writings of Matthew, Paul, and Peter are efficacious and successfully reach the desired outcome.

Local churches throughout the world represent the outworking of this structural composition. It is through their presence, specifically in their gathered assembly, that the people of the world have access to God. This is not to suggest that people engage with God simply by walking into a church service, nor should a faith community take their authority to mean that anything they do or say is an expression of heaven. However, heavenly authority has been given to the body of Christ to wield. Those who seek to know the truth of salvation and God's will for humanity, cannot arrive at a complete outlook on these issues apart from the local church. The Bible clearly links salvation to the faith of the believer, but simultaneously assumes that the faith will be lived out in community.

To proclaim faith apart from the community is to refuse inclusion in the building imagery expressed throughout this book. It is to refrain from wielding the kingdom keys that were handed to the church, and to remove one's self from the priestly duty that the church practices collectively. To isolate one's self assumes too much on their own part, as there is only one cornerstone. All other stones are a part of the spiritually united components that fit together as a house of God. It is in the unity of these saints that many in the world will find their thirst for God and his word. When people from varying national backgrounds and cultural walks of life can merge into a community of love and fellowship, there is a recognizable power at work. The church has expanded through this model for ages, but those who disengage by abandoning the local church disrupt the compelling spirit of Christian unity.

9
Pastoral Insights

THIS BOOK IS THE product of a pastor-theologian. I love the academic side of scholarship and the intense focus that is poured into the various fields of theological studies. However, I am also a pastor who loves to see God use theology to change lives and prompt worship. While many academic works provide theological material with no, or little, application for the reader, the pastor in me does not want to leave it to chance that someone would make it this far in the book and fail to apply the information in a meaningful way. The number of applications that could come from this particular research are legion, and cannot be fully fleshed out in a single chapter. However, there are a few implications that I believe are worthy of special elaboration as we conclude this journey.

THEOLOGICAL IMPLICATIONS OF THE ROCK METAPHOR

The Significance of Christ

If the point was not already sufficiently made, the Bible starts at a high mark with God and his creation, describes the degrading effects of sin, and then works toward a return to the glory of creation in a restoration motif that culminates in the coming of Jesus Christ. The majority of the biblical text focuses, not on the bliss of Eden, but on the restoration of God. Though Christ's appearing *in flesh* does not occur until the NT, the restoration motif of the OT was the scaffolding upon which Jesus' exaltation was gloriously displayed. The rock metaphor is a prime example of a mold filled by the incarnate Son of God. The various strands of the stone testimonia find their fulfillment in Christ. As the premier *telos* of the biblical storyline, Jesus becomes the legitimate focal point of Christian worship. Therefore, the Christian church has every right to make much of Jesus. His supremacy is worthy of every song they can sing, every prayer they can pray, and every faithful sermon they can preach. If he is indeed the cornerstone that holds it all together, there is no *over-doing it* when it comes to worshiping Christ.

The Significance of the Corporate Gathering

In chapter 8, the rock metaphor was used to examine the church and her connection to Christ. This imagery from the stone testimonia indicates that the people of faith are a connected body of rocks united upon the cornerstone of Jesus. The implication is very clear and very simple: faith is lived out in community, not in isolation. Though Western individualism has greatly influenced the Christian church, there is no place for segregation in God's building—i.e., those claiming to be united to Christ independently of the church. Those who have the "I can do it on my own" mentality have not come under the lordship of Jesus, and have thus not built upon the rock of his word. To build on Christ's foundation is to join the multitude of individuals who have realized their inability to save themselves and have thus united to Christ in faith. In the glorious doctrine of *Union with Christ*, the people of God are not just united to Jesus, but also to one another as the body and the temple.

It has been said, "Don't *go* to church, *be* the church," but I think this well-meaning slogan undermines the clear teaching of Scripture. Yes, the church is a people and not a place, but it is a people gathered. Therefore, *going* is an essential part of *being* the church. The Greek word *ekklesia* (church) is defined as "a group or assembly of persons called together for a particular purpose."[1] In light of this definition, *being* the church and *going* to church are not mutually exclusive, but are rather complementary ideas. With this in mind, be the rock you were called to be and join the effort to expand the temple-presence of Christ by gathering with other rocks. Edify one another in the body and find ways to contribute to the growth of the local temple of saints.

---

1. Elwell, *Baker Encyclopedia of the Bible*, 458.

The Significance of Missions and Evangelism

Continuing the idea of temple growth and expansion, the rock metaphor shows us what will happen at the end of the story. The rock expands to the ends of the earth and incorporates people from every nation, tribe, and tongue into its composition. This structure is metaphorically describing Christ's church and his kingdom. Therefore, as Christians we should have the confidence to build and work towards that end. Regardless of what your eschatological commitments are, Christ has given the command to build his temple, to wield the kingdom keys, and to continue the Edenic calling of mankind by filling the world with image bearers of God. Though Adam could have done this through procreation and parenthood, the NT community does this through spiritual procreation and spiritual parenthood, i.e., evangelism and missions. By sharing Christ with the world, the church witnesses the new birth take place in those who respond to the message. Those who join the growing rock of God's kingdom are then built up through discipleship to continue the expansion by their own witness. So whether one believes in an age of evangelistic success that converts the entire world—i.e., *postmillennialism*—or embraces a less optimistic eschatological view, the revealed outcome of the church should compel her to work towards the end result.

The Significance of Place

If the gathering of Christian communities around the world serves as a fulfillment—at least in part—of the expanding rock motif, then it becomes necessary to think in terms of *spatial presence* as believers work out their ecclesiology. The church serves as a picture of Jesus' reign on the earth, where he presides over these corporate gatherings and their priest-king mission. In any area where there is no such gathering, the reign of Christ is absent, leaving the global fulfillment of the expanding rock image underdeveloped—imagine a completed puzzle with a missing piece. Though many await the eschaton for a complete development of this image, it is the responsibility of the church, here and now, to see that it gets as close to fulfillment as possible. While missions and evangelism are a part of this process, the emphasis of spatial occupancy is another important aspect. It has already been stated that *going* to church is an essential part of *being* the church, but the modern climate requires elaboration. Today, many people "go" to church without leaving their house due to the modern ability to pipe church services to homes via the internet and other technological avenues. This use of technology is a blessing for those unable to physically attend and even connects believers to their congregations during times of illness, vacation, and other required travel. Yet, there are many who have used this modern form of church "attendance" as a substitute for gathering *in person*.

Of all the implications listed here, an emphasis on "space" may seem the most foreign. After all, we all take up space regardless of where we are on Sunday morning. The question may emerge, "Can't I just be a part of the expanding rock motif by claiming the spatial parameters of my living room as a manifestation of Christ's kingdom?" And of course the answer to that question could be "yes," if others gathered with you as a church. Yet, if your church is gathering elsewhere, then it is *there* that Christ promises to be in power. It is *there* that the kingdom keys are wielded in adding and subtracting, binding and loosing, opening and shutting. Some churches have succumbed to these arguments and have gone as far as to digitally baptize avatars instead of people, and to provide digital communion instead of physical bread and wine. Unfortunately, the convenience of such practices ends up taking the intended symbolism embedded with these ordinances and distorting it at best, and obliterating it at worst.

Some may read this and dismiss the concern as being just another manifestation of the all too common *fear of change*. Many have criticized the shift from hymnals to the church's use of screens and TVs, resisted contemporary musical arrangements, and acted contentiously towards an assortment of other developments within the church. It is important that the reader understand that my concern for the diminished value on physical attendance is not derived from personal preference nor fear of change. Rather, the issue is based in the theological truths that are derived from Scripture—many of which were highlighted throughout this book—and needs to be thought through with care. When the "gathering" of the church occurs, Christ's reign is magnified as he works among these people in a particular way. The "one another" passages of the church epistles remind the congregations that they have to be interacting with each other in a loving, caring, and unifying way, to properly image Christ in the church. When people refuse to even gather—including those who only choose to participate *digitally*—this brings a blemish to the picture of the church's *being* and Christ's reign. To gather in the fellowship of the Christian community, then, is to live out the reign of Christ in the spatial parameters of that corporate gathering. In a sense, the church *claims the space* of that gathering—whether it's in a church building, a home, or in a park pavilion—as a domain of the new creation. Jesus responds to this gathering by manifesting himself in a unique way to validate their spiritual claim on that portion of creation.

The Significance of the Multiethnic Church

One of the outcomes that is revealed is that the eschatological community in the new heaven and earth is a multiethnic society. How did these diverse people arrive in this final abode? They arrive here because they are all a part of the Christ's church. Paul used the cornerstone motif in Eph 2 to explain how Jews and gentiles were united together in the fellowship of the Christian community. This was not a one-off incident, but was an ecclesiological pattern established for every church to mimic. If Jesus is the cornerstone that can unite Jew and gentile, then it is the cornerstone that can unite all ethnic and cultural backgrounds into one unified body. There is then no grounds for partiality, social or racial segregation, or any other schism in the community of rocks. The church, as an expanding edifice, is a rock *not made by human hands*, and should, therefore, reflect the power of God through unity.

If I have not been specific enough on this point, let it be stated that the rock metaphor compels us to sow the seed of the gospel to all people in our local setting. If that setting is one that is racially diverse, then the seed we sow in evangelism and missions should be dispersed without partiality. If our communities are made up of those representing the wealthy, poor, and middle class, our duty is to sow the seed among them all without favoring one socioeconomic group over another. Not only is this our duty in evangelism, but also our responsibility as we establish our ecclesiological polity. Peter and Paul depict a temple built of stones but they do not emphasize any distinction in these stones in relationship to their racial background, financial resources, or social status. Those who emphasize these qualities over the biblical criteria for church membership, leadership, and ministerial involvement do so to the detriment of the church's health. If the church is God's building, believers need to maintain its integrity by submitting to the divine order given in Scripture rather than the template of the world.

Pastoral Insights

The Significance of the Priesthood of Every Believer

Throughout the previous chapters, a heavy emphasis has been placed on the priest-king duty that was given to Adam but fulfilled in Christ. Additionally, a heavy emphasis has been placed on the doctrine of *union with Christ* which is the basis for humanity's participation if the fulfillment of this priest-king responsibility. Though the terms of "king" and "priest" are used in very distinct ways in the OT, and are therefore designated to particular people, those divisions and distinctions disappear in the kingdom of God. The rock metaphor describes the church as a collection of rocks stacked upon one foundation in Christ Jesus. It further depicts each believer as *living stones* that make up a holy priesthood. Therefore, every believer has been commissioned as priest-kings, regardless of age, ethnic background, social status, or gender. In Gal 3:28 Paul explains that there is neither "Jew nor Greek, there is neither slave nor free, there is no male and female, for you are all one in Christ Jesus." This verse does not mean that these distinctions are totally absent in every way, but does suggest that inclusion in Christ is not affected by these differences. Jesus' commission to "make disciples" does not lie in the hands of a few chosen individuals of a particular pedigree, but rather is extended to every stone in the new temple of God. Arguments can be made for certain theological positions that necessitate an ongoing distinction between these categories—e.g., complementarianism for gender, and dispensationalism for race—however, these positions are not debating *who* as much as they are answering *how* and *when*. For serious students of Scripture, there should be a consensus that *all believers* are priest-kings as a direct result of their union with Christ.

The Significance of Biblical Theology for the Church

There has been a bit of confusion regarding how the NT community should interact with the OT Scripture. In recent years, there have been numerous proposals as to how the OT should be dealt with. While some of these proposals have been helpful, others have been outright heretical. By walking the reader through the Scriptures and showing them how the OT message connects to the revelation of the NT, my hope is that the Bible would be recognized as a unified whole, rather than a two-part literary composition. The work of tracing themes through the biblical corpus yields the reward of seeing the continuity of thematic patterns that find no resolution when the OT and NT are treated as separate literary units. While I firmly believe that the OT text had merit in its own right for the faith community of the old covenant, I believe the significance of those texts became amplified and clarified in the fulfillment of Christ. The church that ignores the teaching of the OT loses the unified storyline of God and the grandiose accomplishment of Christ in this fulfillment.

Bibliography

Abegg, Martin G., et al. *The Dead Sea Scrolls Bible: The Oldest Known Bible Translated for the First Time into English*. Repr. ed. San Francisco, CA: HarperOne, 2002.
Akright, Brett. "A Critical Examination of the Role of 'In Christ' in Ephesians 1–3: A Proposal for Interpreting 'In Christ' within Its Epistolary Cotext and Context." PhD diss., Midwestern Baptist Theological Seminary, 2019.
Albright, William Foxwell. *Yahweh and the Gods of Canaan: A Historical Analysis of Two Contrasting Faiths*. Jordan Lectures in Comparative Religion 7. London: Athlone, 1968.
Alexander, T. Desmond. *From Eden to the New Jerusalem: An Introduction to Biblical Theology*. Grand Rapids: Kregel Academic & Professional, 2009.
———. "Royal Expectations in Genesis to Kings: Their Importance for Biblical Theology." *Tyndale Bulletin* 49.2 (1998) 191–212.
Alexander, T. Desmond, et al. *The City of God and the Goal of Creation*. Wheaton, IL: Crossway, 2018.
Allen, Clifton J. *Broadman Bible Commentary: Matthew and Mark*. Vol 8. London: Marshall, Morgan & Scott, 1970.
Archer, Gleason. *A Survey of Old Testament Introduction*. Rev., updated ed. Chicago: Moody, 1996.
Barber, Michael Patrick. "Jesus as the Davidic Temple Builder and Peter's Priestly Role in Matthew 16:16–19." *Journal of Biblical Literature* 132.4 (2013) 935–53.
Barker, Margaret. *Temple Themes in Christian Worship*. New York: T&T Clark, 2008.
———. *Temple Theology: An Introduction*. SPCK, 2004.
Barrett, Matthew, and D. A. Carson. *Canon, Covenant and Christology: Rethinking Jesus and the Scriptures of Israel*. Downers Grove, IL: IVP Academic, 2020.
Bartholomew, Craig G. *Where Mortals Dwell: A Christian View of Place for Today*. Grand Rapids: Baker Academic, 2011.
Barton, John. "'The Work of Human Hands' (Ps 115:4): Idolatry in the Old Testament; Ex Auditu." *Ex Auditu* 15 (1999) 63–72.
Bauer, Walter, et al., eds. *A Greek-English Lexicon of the New Testament and Other Early Christian Literature*. 3rd ed. Chicago: University of Chicago Press, 2001.
Beale, G. K. *The Book of Revelation*. New International Greek Testament Commentary. Grand Rapids: Eerdmans, 1998.

Bibliography

———. "Eden, the Temple, and the Church's Mission in the New Creation." *Journal of the Evangelical Theological Society* 48.1 (March 2005) 5–31.

———. *Handbook on the New Testament Use of the Old Testament: Exegesis and Interpretation*. Grand Rapids: Baker, 2012.

———. *A New Testament Biblical Theology: The Unfolding of the Old Testament in the New*. Grand Rapids: Baker Academic, 2011.

———. *The Temple and the Church's Mission: A Biblical Theology of the Dwelling Place of God*. Downers Grove, IL: IVP Academic, 2004.

Beale, G. K., and Mitchell Kim. *God Dwells among Us: Expanding Eden to the Ends of the Earth*. Downers Grove, IL: IVP, 2014.

Beeke, Joel R., and Paul M. Smalley. "Images of Union and Communion with Christ." *Puritan Reformed Journal* 8.2 (July 2016) 125–36.

Ben Shahar, Meir. "'Anointed' and 'Messiah': A New Investigation into an Old Problem." *Journal for the Study of the Old Testament* 42.4 (June 2018) 393–413.

Berlin, Adele. *The Dynamics of Biblical Parallelism*. Grand Rapids: Eerdmans, 2008.

Blomberg, Craig L. *Matthew: An Exegetical and Theological Exposition of Holy Scripture*. Vol. 22. The New American Commentary. Nashville: B&H, 1992.

Bock, Darrell L., et al. *Ephesians: An Introduction and Commentary*. 1st ed. Downers Grove, IL: IVP Academic, 2019.

Brueggemann, Walter. *The Land: Place as Gift, Promise, and Challenge in Biblical Faith*. 2nd ed. Minneapolis: Augsburg, 2002.

Cahill, Michael. "Not a Cornerstone! Translating Ps 118:22 in the Jewish and Christian Scriptures." *Revue Biblique* 106.3 (1999) 345–57.

Campbell, Constantine R. *Paul and Union with Christ: An Exegetical and Theological Study*. Grand Rapids: Zondervan Academic, 2015.

Gaebelein, Frank E., et al. *The Expositor's Bible Commentary: Matthew, Mark, Luke*. Vol. 8. Grand Rapids: Zondervan, 1984.

Carson, D. A. *The Gospel according to John*. The Pillar New Testament Commentary. Leicester: Inter-Varsity, 1991.

Carson, D. A., and G. K. Beale, eds. *Commentary on the New Testament Use of the Old Testament*. Grand Rapids: Baker Academic, 2007.

Carson, D. A., et al. *The Expositor's Bible Commentary: Matthew, Mark, Luke, with the New International Version of the Holy Bible*. Edited by Frank E. Gaebelein. London: Zondervan, 1984.

Charlesworth, James H. *The Old Testament Pseudepigrapha and the New Testament: Expansions of the "Old Testament" and Legends, Wisdom, and Philosophical Literature, Prayers, Psalms and Odes, Fragments of Lost Judeo-Hellenistic Works*. Vol. 2. New Haven, CT: Yale University Press, 1985.

———. *The Old Testament Pseudepigrapha*. Vol. 1. New York: Yale University Press, 1983.

Childs, Brevard S. *Isaiah: A Commentary*. 1st ed. Louisville: Westminster John Knox, 2000.

Christensen, Sean M. "Reborn Participants in Christ: Recovering the Importance of Union with Christ in 1 Peter." *Journal of the Evangelical Theological Society* 61.2 (June 2018) 339–54.

Crawford, Greg Anthony. *Where Has Sacred Space Gone? Exploring the Temple-Presence of God in the Church Assembly*. PhD diss., Midwestern Baptist Theological Seminary, 2021.

Bibliography

Davies, W. D., and Dale Allison. *Matthew 8–18*. Vol. 2. International Critical Commentary. New York: T&T Clark International, 2004.

Dempster, Stephen G. *Dominion and Dynasty: A Theology of the Hebrew Bible*. Edited by D. A. Carson. Downers Grove, IL: IVP Academic, 2003.

Domeris, Bill. "God, Our Rock (Deut 32:1–43): Reading the Metaphor in Its Pentateuchal Context." *Conspectus* 30 (October 2020) 20–33.

Duling, Dennis C. "Solomon, Exorcism, and the Son of David." *Harvard Theological Review* 68.3–4 (July 1975) 235–52.

Elwell, Walter A. *Baker Encyclopedia of the Bible*. Vol. 2, J–Z. Grand Rapids: Baker, 1988.

Emerson, Matthew Y. *Christ and the New Creation: A Canonical Approach to the Theology of the New Testament*. Eugene, OR: Wipf & Stock, 2013.

Enns, Peter. "The 'Moveable Well' in 1 Cor 10:4: An Extrabiblical Tradition in an Apostolic Text." *Bulletin for Biblical Research* 6 (1996) 23–38.

Fee, Gordon D. *The First Epistle to the Corinthians*. Revised edition. Grand Rapids: Eerdmans, 2014.

Floyd, Richard C. "The Concept of Discipleship in Deuteronomy: Literary and Lexical Insights into Following YHWH." *Journal for the Evangelical Study of the Old Testament* 7.2 (2021) 37–71.

Foulkes, Francis. *Ephesians*. Tyndale New Testament Commentaries 10. Grand Rapids: Eerdmans, 1989.

France, R. T. *Matthew: An Introduction and Commentary*. Tyndale New Testament Commentaries 1. Nottingham: IVP, 2008.

———. *The Gospel of Mark*. Grand Rapids: Eerdmans, 2002.

———. *The Gospel of Matthew*. The New International Commentary on the New Testament. Grand Rapids: Eerdmans, 2007.

Freeman, Brandon. "The Church's One Foundation: The Stone Metaphor And Its Theological Significance." PhD diss., Midwestern Baptist Theological Seminary, 2023.

Gangel, Kenneth. *John*. Edited by Max Anders. Holman New Testament Commentary. Nashville: Holman Reference, 2000.

García Martínez, Florentino, and Eibert J. C. Tigchelaar. *The Dead Sea Scrolls Study Edition (Translations)*. 2 vols. New York: Brill, 1997.

Garland, David E. *2 Corinthians*. New American Commentary 29. Nashville: B&H, 1999.

Gentry, Peter J., and Stephen J. Wellum. *God's Kingdom through God's Covenants: A Concise Biblical Theology*. 1st ed. Crossway, 2015.

Goldingay, John. *Psalms*. Vol. 1, *Psalms 1–41*, edited by Tremper Longman III. Illustrated ed. Baker Commentary on the Old Testament Wisdom and Psalms. Baker Academic, 2006.

Gonzalez, Eliezer. "Jesus and the Temple in John and Hebrews: Towards a New Testament Perspective." *DavarLogos* 15.2 (2016) 39–65.

Greene, Joseph R. "The Spirit in the Temple: Bridging the Gap Between Old Testament Absence and New Testament Assumption." *Journal of the Evangelical Theological Society* 55.4 (December 2012) 717–42.

Green, Joel B. *1 Peter*. Two Horizons New Testament Commentary. Grand Rapids: Eerdmans, 2007.

Grudem, Wayne A. *1 Peter: An Introduction and Commentary*. Tyndale New Testament Commentaries 17. Downers Grove, IL: IVP Academic, 2009.

Bibliography

———. *Systematic Theology: An Introduction to Biblical Doctrine*. Grand Rapids: Zondervan Academic, 1994.

Guenter, Kenneth E. "'Blessed Is He Who Comes': Psalm 118 and Jesus's Triumphal Entry." *Bibliotheca Sacra* 173.692 (October 2016) 425–47.

Gupta, Nijay K. "A Spiritual House of Royal Priests, Chosen and Honored: The Presence and Function of Cultic Imagery in 1 Peter." *Perspectives in Religious Studies* 36.1 (2009) 61–76.

———. "Which 'Body' Is a Temple (1 Corinthians 6:19)?: Paul beyond the Individual/Communal Divide." *The Catholic Biblical Quarterly* 72.3 (July 2010) 518–36.

Hagner, Donald Alfred. *Matthew 14–28*. Vol. 33B. Word Biblical Commentary. Grand Rapids: Zondervan, 2010.

Hays, J. Daniel. *The Temple and the Tabernacle: A Study of God's Dwelling Places from Genesis to Revelation*. Grand Rapids: Baker, 2016.

Hearson, Blake N. "Bethel: Where Is the House of God? Defining Sacred Space in the Bible." *Midwestern Journal of Theology* 15.1 (2016) 66–83.

———. *Go Now to Shiloh: A Biblical Theology of Sacred Space*. Nashville: B&H Academic, 2020.

Henry, Matthew, and Thomas Scott. *Matthew Henry Concise Commentary on the Whole Bible*. Logos Research ed. Oak Harbor, WA: Logos Research Systems, 1997.

Hill, Andrew E., et al. *Daniel–Malachi*. Edited by Tremper Longman III and David E. Garland. Rev. ed. Grand Rapids: Zondervan Academic, 2008.

Hjalmarson, Leonard. *No Home Like Place: A Christian Theology of Place*. Portland: Urban Loft, 2015.

Hodge, Charles. *Systematic Theology*. Oak Harbor, WA: Logos Research Systems, 1997.

Hoehner, Harold W. *Ephesians: An Exegetical Commentary*. Grand Rapids: Baker Academic, 2002.

Hooker, Morna D. "'The Sanctuary of His Body': Body and Sanctuary in Paul and John." *Journal for the Study of the New Testament* 39.4 (2017) 347–61.

Hoskins, Paul M. *Jesus as the Fulfillment of the Temple in the Gospel of John*. Eugene, OR: Wipf & Stock, 2007.

House, Paul R. *1, 2 Kings: An Exegetical and Theological Exposition of Holy Scripture*. Nashville: Holman Reference, 1995.

Inge, John. *A Christian Theology of Place*. Aldershot, England: Routledge, 2003.

Johann Maier. *The Temple Scroll: An Introduction, Translation and Commentary*. Journal for the Study of the Old Testament Supplement Series. Sheffield: Sheffield Academic, 1985.

Joseph, Simon J. *Jesus and the Temple: The Crucifixion in Its Jewish Context*. Repr. ed. United Kingdom: Cambridge University Press, 2018.

Josephus, Flavius, and William Whiston. *The Works of Josephus: Complete and Unabridged*. New updated ed. Peabody, MA: Hendrickson, 1987.

Nataf, R. Francis, ed. "Midrash Tanchuma, Kedoshim 10." Sefaria, n.d. https://www.sefaria.org/Midrash_Tanchuma%2C_Kedoshim.10?lang=bi.

Keel, Othmar. *The Symbolism of the Biblical World: Ancient Near Eastern Iconography and the Book of Psalms*. Seabury, NY: 1978.

Keener, Craig S. "One New Temple in Christ (Ephesians 2:11–22; Acts 21:27–29; Mark 11:17; John 4:20–24)." *Asian Journal of Pentecostal Studies* 12.1 (January 2009) 75–92.

Kent, Homer A Jr. "Matthew's Use of the Old Testament." *Bibliotheca Sacra* 121.481 (January 1964) 34–43.

Bibliography

Kerr, Alan. *The Temple of Jesus' Body: The Temple Theme in the Gospel of John*. London: Sheffield Academic, 2002.

Kirk, David R. "When You Come Together: Gathered Worship in the New Testament: Foundations An International Journal of Evangelical Theology." *Foundations: An International Journal of Evangelical Theology* 76 (Spring 2019) 34–60.

Kittel, Gerhard, and Gerhard Friedrich. *Theological Dictionary of the New Testament*. Vol. 9. Grand Rapids: Eerdmans, 1973.

Klein, George. *Zechariah: An Exegetical and Theological Exposition of Holy Scripture*. The New American Commentary 21B. Nashville: B&H Publishing, 2008.

Ladd, George Eldon. *Gospel of the Kingdom: Scriptural Studies in the Kingdom of God*. Grand Rapids: Eerdmans, 1990.

———. *A Theology of the New Testament*. Grand Rapids: Eerdmans, 1993.

Lanier, Gregory R. "The Rejected Stone in the Parable of the Wicked Tenants: Defending the Authenticity of Jesus' Quotation of Ps 118:22." *Journal of the Evangelical Theological Society* 56.4 (December 2013) 733–51.

Lanier, Gregory R., and Chris Keith. *Old Testament Conceptual Metaphors and the Christology of Luke's Gospel*. New York: T&T Clark, 2018.

Leeman, Jonathan. *Political Church: The Local Assembly as Embassy of Christ's Rule*. Downers Grove, IL: IVP Academic, 2016.

Leithart, Peter J. *The Gospel of Matthew through New Eyes*. Vol. 1, *Jesus as Israel*. West Monroe, LA: Athanasius, 2018.

Levenson, Jon D. *Sinai and Zion*. Cambridge: HarperOne, 1987.

———. "The Temple and the World." *The Journal of Religion* 64.3 (1984) 275–98.

Lioy, Daniel T. "The Garden of Eden as a Primordial Temple or Sacred Space for Humankind." *Conspectus* 10 (September 2010) 25–57.

Liu, Yulin. *Temple Purity in 1–2 Corinthians*. Wissenschaftliche Untersuchungen Zum Neuen Testament 2. Reihe 343. Tübingen: Mohr Siebeck, 2013.

Longman, Tremper, III, and David E. Garland, eds. *The Expositor's Bible Commentary: Daniel–Malachi*. Vol. 8. Rev ed. Grand Rapids: Zondervan, 2008.

———, eds. *The Expositor's Bible Commentary: Psalms*. Vol. 5. Rev ed. Grand Rapids: Zondervan, 2008.

Marshall, I. Howard. "Church and Temple in the New Testament." *Tyndale Bulletin* 40.2 (November 1989) 203–22.

Marshall, I. Howard, et al., eds. *New Bible Dictionary*. 3rd ed. Downers Grove, IL: IVP Academic, 1996.

Marshall, John S. "'A Spiritual House an Holy Priesthood' (1 Peter Ii.5)." *Anglican Theological Review* 28.4 (October 1946) 227–28.

Marsh, Cory M. "On Account of My Name: An Ecclesial Shift through Righteous Suffering in John 15–16." *JETS* 66.4 (2023) 671–84.

Martin, Oren. *Bound for the Promised Land*. Downers Grove, IL: IVP Academic, 2015.

Martin, Ralph P., and Peter H. Davids, eds. *Dictionary of the Later New Testament and Its Developments*. Downers Grove, IL: IVP Academic, 1998.

Mbuvi, Andrew Mutua. *Temple, Exile and Identity in 1 Peter*. London: T&T Clark, 2007.

McGlynn, Moyna. "Authority and Sacred Space: Concepts of the Jerusalem Temple in Aristeas, Wisdom, and Josephus." *Biblische Notizen* 161 (2014) 115–40.

McKelvey, R. J. "Christ the Cornerstone." *New Testament Studies* 8.4 (1962) 352–59.

Minear, Paul S. "The House of Living Stones: A Study of 1 Peter 2:4–12." *Ecumenical Review* 34.3 (July 1982) 238–48.

Bibliography

Moo, Douglas J. *The Letter to the Romans*. 2nd ed. Grand Rapids: Eerdmans, 2018.

Motyer, J. A. *The Prophecy of Isaiah: An Introduction and Commentary*. Downers Grove, IL: InterVarsity, 1996.

Neusner, Jacob. *The Babylonian Talmud: A Translation and Commentary*. 22 vols. Peabody, MA: Hendrickson, 2011.

Niehaus, Jeffrey J. *Ancient Near Eastern Themes in Biblical Theology*. Grand Rapids: Kregel Academic & Professional, 2008.

Osborne, Grant R. *Revelation*. Baker Exegetical Commentary on the New Testament. Grand Rapids: Baker Academic, 2002.

Oswalt, John N. *The Book of Isaiah, Chapters 1–39*. New International Commentary On The Old Testament. Grand Rapids: Eerdmans, 1986.

Otto, Rudolf. *The Idea of the Holy: Text of First English Edition*. Eastford, CT: Martino, 2010.

Ouro, Roberto. "Divine Presence Theology Versus Name Theology in Deuteronomy." *Andrews University Seminary Studies* 52.1 (2014) 5–29.

Perrin, Nicholas. "Jesus as Priest in the Gospels." *The Southern Baptist Journal of Theology* 22.2 (2018) 81–99.

Philo of Alexandria. *The Works of Philo*. Peabody, MA: Hendrickson, 1993.

Potts, Donald R. "Samaria, Samaritans." In *Holman Illustrated Bible Dictionary*, edited by Chad Brand et al., 1435–37. Nashville: Holman, 2003.

Powell, Mark Allan. "Binding and Loosing: A Paradigm for Ethical Discernment from the Gospel of Matthew." *Currents in Theology and Mission* 30.6 (2003) 438–45.

Pula, Melissa. "Rethinking the Community as Temple: Discourse and Spatial Practice in the Community Rule (1QS)." PhD diss. University of Denver, 2015.

Quarles, Charles L. *A Theology of Matthew: Jesus Revealed as Deliverer, King, and Incarnate Creator*. Explorations in Biblical Theology. Phillipsburg, NJ: P&R, 2013.

Regev, Eyal. "Abominated Temple and a Holy Community: The Formation of the Notions of Purity and Impurity in Qumran." *Dead Sea Discoveries* 10.2 (Jan 1, 2003) 243–78.

———. "Community as Temple: Revisiting Cultic Metaphors in Qumran and the New Testament." *Bulletin for Biblical Research* 28.4 (2018) 604–31.

———. "Moral Impurity and the Temple in Early Christianity in Light of Ancient Greek Practice and Qumranic Ideology." *Harvard Theological Review* 97.4 (October 2004) 383–411.

———. *Sectarianism in Qumran: A Cross-Cultural Perspective*. Religion and Society 45. Berlin; New York: Walter de Gruyter, 2007.

———. *The Temple in Early Christianity: Experiencing the Sacred*. New Haven, CT: Yale University Press, 2019.

Sarna, Nahum M. *The JPS Torah Commentary: Exodus*. 1st ed. Philadelphia, PA: Jewish Publication Society, 1991.

Schreiner, Patrick. *The Body of Jesus: A Spatial Analysis of the Kingdom in Matthew*. New York: Bloomsbury T&T Clark, 2016.

———. "Peter, the Rock: Matthew 16 in Light of Daniel 2." *Criswell Theological Review* 2 (2016) 99–117.

Schreiner, Thomas R. *1, 2 Peter, Jude*. The New American Commentary 37. Nashville: Broadman & Holman, 2003.

———. *The King in His Beauty: A Biblical Theology of the Old and New Testaments*. Grand Rapids: Baker Academic, 2013.

Bibliography

———. *New Testament Theology: Magnifying God in Christ*. Grand Rapids: Baker Academic, 2008.

———. *Paul, Apostle of God's Glory in Christ: A Pauline Theology*. Grand Rapids: IVP Academic, 2006.

Sklar, Jay. *Leviticus: An Introduction and Commentary*. Tyndale Old Testament Commentaries. Downers Grove, IL: IVP Academic, 2014.

Smith, Gary V. *Isaiah 1–39*. Edited by E. Ray Clendenen. Vol. 15A. The New American Commentary. Nashville: Broadman & Holman, 2007.

Smith, Stephen C. *The House of the Lord: A Catholic Biblical Theology of God's Temple Presence in the Old and New Testaments*. Steubenville, OH: Franciscan University Press, 2017.

Snodgrass, Klyne Ryland. "The Christological Stone Testimonia in the New Testament." PhD diss., University of St. Andrews, 1973.

Storms, Sam. *Kingdom Come: The Amillennial Alternative*. Rev. ed. Fearn, UK: Mentor, 2015.

Thiessen, Matthew. "'The Rock Was Christ': The Fluidity of Christ's Body in I Corinthians 10.4." *Journal for the Study of the New Testament* 36.2 (December 2013) 103–26.

Thiselton, Anthony C. *The First Epistle to the Corinthians*. New International Greek Testament Commentary. Grand Rapids: Eerdmans, 2000.

Thompson, J. A. *1, 2 Chronicles*. Nashville: Holman Reference, 1994.

Truex, Jerry. "God's Spiritual House: A Study of 1 Peter 2:4–5." *Direction* 33.2 (2004) 185–93.

Vaillancourt, Ian J. "Psalm 118 and the Eschatological Son of David." *Journal of the Evangelical Theological Society* 62.4 (December 2019) 721–38.

Vance, Alan B. "The Church as the New Temple in Matthew 16:17–19: A Biblical-Theological Consideration of Jesus' Response to Peter's Confession as Recorded by Matthew." Master's thesis, Gordon-Conwell Theological Seminary, 1992.

Vanhoozer, Kevin J. *The Drama of Doctrine: A Canonical Linguistic Approach to Christian Doctrine*. Louisville: Westminster John Knox, 2005.

Verbrugge, Verlyn, ed. *New International Dictionary of New Testament Theology*. Abridged ed. Grand Rapids: Zondervan Academic, 2003.

———. "The Power to Bind and Loose" *Reformed Journal* 30.7 (July 1980) 15–17.

Vermes, Geza. *The Complete Dead Sea Scrolls In English*. Rev. ed. London: Penguin, 2004.

Vos, Geerhardus. "Eschatology of the Psalter." *The Princeton Theological Review* 18 (January 1920) 1–43.

Wellum, Stephen J., and John S. Feinberg. *God the Son Incarnate: The Doctrine of Christ*. Crossway, 2016.

Wheeler, Nathan. "'For a Holy Priesthood': A Petrine Model for Evangelical Cultural Engagement." *Journal of the Evangelical Theological Society* 59.3 (September 2016) 523–39.

Wilcox, Max. "Peter and the Rock: A Fresh Look at Matthew 16:17–19." *New Testament Studies* 22.1 (October 1975) 73–88.

Wise, Michael O., et al. *The Dead Sea Scrolls: A New Translation*. Rev. ed. New York: HarperOne, 2005.

Witt, Andrew. "Hearing Psalm 102 within the Context of the Hebrew Psalter." *Vetus Testamentum* 62.4 (2012) 582–606.

Woods, Edward J. *Deuteronomy: An Introduction and Commentary*. Downers Grove, IL: IVP Acedemic, 2011.

Bibliography

Wright, N. T. "Jerusalem in the New Testament." In *Jerusalem: Past and Present in the Purposes of God*, subsequent ed., edited by Peter W. L. Walker, 53–77. Grand Rapids: Cambridge University Press, 1994.

———. *The New Testament and the People of God*. 1st North American ed. Minneapolis: Fortress, 1992.

Youngblood, Ronald F., et al. *1 Samuel–2 Kings*. Edited by Tremper Longman III and David E. Garland. Rev. ed. Grand Rapids: Zondervan Academic, 2010.

Ancient Document Index

Genesis

1:2	38–39
1:26	53
2	47
2:10–14	34, 110
2:11–12	36
3:22–24	36
11	35
18:25	41
22	45
28	49
28:18	1
31:13	49
35:1–15	49
48:15	41
49:24	41

Exodus

3	31
3:5	31
3:12	31, 111
14:11	32
15:17	31
17	33
17:6	13, 32–33
17:12	1
19:6	31, 64, 101, 106
19:12	33, 36
20:11	50
20:25	68
23:24–25	31
26:33	36
26:34–35	108
27:21	104
28:9–12	108
28:15–30	47, 110
28:36–38	111
29:46	91
31:18	1
33:21	33
33:22	1

Leviticus

14	88
14:1–20	88
16:2	36
17:10–14	104

Numbers

16:9	112
19:20	104

Deuteronomy

4	10
4:24	41
4:25–28	11
4:28	67
8:19	31
10:2–5	1
10:12	31
10:20	31

Ancient Document Index

Deuteronomy (*cont.*)

12:5–6	28
18:15	84
28:47–48	31
30:17–18	20
32	44
32:4	41, 45
32:6	41
32:15	42, 46
32:18	41–43
32:30	42
32:31	42

Joshua

22:25	31
22:29	79
24:16–31	31

Judges

2:11–13	31
21:2	49

1 Samuel

2:2	42
7:10–11a	60
8:20	53
10:19	53
13:8–14	79
16:13	55
16:23	82
17:50	1
22:17–18	81

2 Samuel

7:12–16	58
7:14	83, 84
22	42, 44
22:2b	42
22:3	1
23:3	42
24:25	79

1 Kings

3:2–3	28
3:15	79
6:7	67
8:9	1
8:27–30	28
8:27	67
13:32	28
18:20–40	34

2 Kings

16:7–9	19
15:28	20

1 Chronicles

22:2	1
22:8	58
29:2	47, 87

2 Chronicles

2:12	56
3:1	46
23:19	91
28:22–27	28
36:23	69, 92

Job

38:6	37

Psalms

1:1–3	40
2:6–7	56
2:7	55, 83, 84
3	58
7	58
8:6	84
18	58
18:2	42–43, 46
18:31	42
18:46	42
19:14	42
22:1	82
28:1	42
31:2–3	42
40:2	45
42:1	40
42:9	42
48:1	109

50:1–2	37	7	19
51:11	55	7:14	54–56
62:2	42, 46	8	22–25, 30, 94
62:6	42	8:5–10	20–21
72:1	55, 83	8:8	20
78:20	46	8:10	21
78:56–72	28	8:14–15	18–19, 22, 25
89:20–26	55	8:14	13, 18–19, 88
89:26	46	8:18	13, 19
93:1	62	9:6–7	69, 83
97:7–8	28	9:8–21	20
100:2	31	10:10–12	28
102	72–73	11:1–10	69
102:26	72	17:10	43
105:41	46	18:7	56
110:2–4	79	22:22–25	58
114:8	46	22:22	91
115:4	67	26:4	43, 45
118	11, 24–25, 38, 56, 94	28	22–23, 30, 62
		28:2	23
118:14	25	28:16	18, 22, 25, 62, 88
118:19–20	24	28:17	23
118:22	18, 24–25, 54–59, 62, 86, 88	30	30
		30:28	30
118:23	25	30:29	30
118:25–26	56	40	75
118:27	25, 56	40:9	109
135:15	67	44:8	43
		48:21	46
Proverbs		51:1–2	47
11:25	40	55:1–3	40
		57:13	28
Isaiah		**Jeremiah**	
1:12	21	8:19	28
2	71	48:13	49
2:1–22	28		
2:2	71	**Ezekiel**	
2:3	71	1:26–28	110
2:4–5	71	28:13–14	35
2:10	72	28:13	47, 110
2:14–15	72	40:2	109
2:19	72	43:7	28
2:21	72	47	61
2:22	72	47:1–12	35, 38
5	57		

Ancient Document Index

Daniel
2	65, 68–70, 73, 94, 112
2:31–45	1, 101
2:34–35	65
2:34	68
2:35	69
2:36–38	69
2:38	66
2:44–45	70
2:44	65
7:13–14	75
7:13	68
7:14	68
7:18	68

Hosea
10:15	49

Amos
4:4	49
9:11–12	61
9:11	60

Micah
1:1–16	28

Habakkuk
1:12	43, 45

Zechariah
3:9	85
4:10	85–86, 108
6:12–13	58
6:13–14	79
10:3–4	54, 58
10:4	59

Bel and the Dragon
15:5	67

2 Baruch
39–40	70
40:3	70

2 Enoch
22:2	66
33:4–7	66

4 Ezra
2:34–35	70
13:33–36	73
13:44–45	74

Matthew
1	82
1:23	91
3:2–3	75
6:10	100
7	9, 10–11, 22, 97–98, 100
7:24–27	10, 47, 96–97
7:24	83
12:28	97
13:31–33	75, 100
16	11, 14, 90–91, 97–100
16:16–19	47, 90–91, 96–98, 103
16:16–18	83
16:16	83
16:18–19	98
16:18	11, 97–98, 106
16:19	90, 103
16:23	99
18	103
18:6	9
18:15–20	98, 103
18:18–20	91
18:18	90, 103
18:20	103–4
21	38, 57, 60, 97, 100
21:9	56
21:12–46	97
21:12	57
21:13	38
21:21	39
21:23	57
21:42–44	25
21:42	11, 96, 100
21:43–45	100

21:43	57	15:4	106
21:44	18	17:24	95
24	39, 57, 75		
24:2	97	**Acts**	
24:30–31	75	15	61
24:36	76	17:24–25	67
26:26–29	98		
26:63	84	**1 Corinthians**	
28:18–20	92	1:23	18
28:18	97	3	86–87
28:20	91	3:9–16	61
		3:11–13	87
Mark		3:11	8, 12
1:11	83	3:16–17	101–2, 104
9:7	84	3:16	22, 101
10:47	82	5:4–5	104
14	68	5:4	104
14:58	68	5:7	85
14:61	68	6:19	22, 102, 104
14:62	68	10	13–14
15:32	84	10:4	8, 14, 32
		10:12	14
Luke		10:23	14
1:32–33	70		
2:11	82	**2 Corinthians**	
3	82	6:16	102
6:46	83		
23:53	8	**Galatians**	
24:2	8	3:28	119
24:27	8, 55		
		Ephesians	
John		1:4	95
1:1–4	60, 93	1:20	106
1:14	60–61	1:21	84
1:29	85	1:22	84
1:36	85	2	62, 118
1:51	17, 61	2:6	106
2:13–22	18	2:11–22	102
2:19	61	2:13–16	88
2:21	61	2:14–22	61
2:22	90	2:14	88, 102
4	18, 29	2:15	88
4:20	29	2:16	88
4:22	29	2:17	88
7:38	61	2:19–22	25
12:16	90		

Ephesians (cont.)

2:19–21	12
2:19	84
2:20–22	87–88
2:20	84, 99
2:22	14
5:2	88
5:26–27	88
5:26	88

Colossians

1:16	93

Hebrews

1:3	93

1 Peter

1:1	107
1:15–16	105
1:15	105
1:18–19	88
1:19	85, 105
1:20	95
2	105
2:1–12	105
2:1–10	62, 85, 88
2:4–8	15
2:4–5	25, 99
2:4	105
2:5	22, 106
2:6–8	8
2:6–7	59, 105
2:6	105
2:7–8	18
2:8	22, 85
2:9	22, 62, 85
2:24	105
3:15	105

Revelation

1:5	107
2:17	8, 108
3:12	108
4:2–3	110
5	85, 89, 108
5:5	82, 85
5:6	85
5:9–10	108
5:9	85
5:10	85, 89
7:9	108
11:15	70
15:4	50
20:6	108
21	69, 109,
21:1–3	69
21:1	38
21:10	109
21:12–14	111
21:14	99
21:19–20	109
21:22	35, 110, 112
21:23	112
21:24	108, 111
22:1–2	35, 38
22:3–5	111
22:16	82

Dead Sea Scrolls

1QHa	43
1QpHab	43
1QS	43, 74, 80
1Q28b	74
11Q5	73
11Q19	74
4Q174	60
4Q246	70
4Q254	43
4Q377	43
4Q381	43
4Q504	43
4Q522	29–30, 59
4QMMT	74

Rabbinic Literature

b. Berakhot	43
b. Menahot	43–44
b. Sanhedrin	40
b. Yoma	37